Skill Builders

**Leadership Tools
for Opening Doors
to Your Community**

TCN
TRANSFORMING
CHURCHES
NETWORK

Table of Contents

Introduction

In the opening scene of the *Get Smart* movie, Maxwell Smart is shown walking through a variety of mechanical doors that close behind him as soon as he steps through them. In much the same way, the American Church is seeing doors that were once open and inviting now closing rapidly and soundly. These church doors are both literal and figurative. Sadly, many churches are closing the doors of their buildings for the last time, as the communities around them deem these churches irrelevant. For most churches though, this image of closed doors is figurative. For them, the tried and true doors they used to engage people in the community in the past are now becoming smaller and smaller or simply no longer open at all.

Transforming Churches Network has surveyed thousands of people in small to medium-sized churches in America that are seeking to open doors to the community. The results of the research indicate clearly that there are eight behavioral drivers that will transform an inwardly-focused church. The research demonstrates which factors, or "hinges," have the greatest impact on opening doors. Utilizing these hinges results in meaningful community engagement with opportunities for demonstrating and sharing the love of Jesus Christ with those who need to hear and experience the message of the Gospel.

The use of these hinges depends upon the development of new skills. Much like shooting a left-handed lay-up, installing a sink, or tweeting, these are skills that almost anyone can develop. Now granted, no matter how many hours you spend in the gym shooting lay-ups, you will likely never become the next Michael Jordan; and no matter how many bathroom floors you flood, you will never be mistaken for Bob Vila. Even so, practice will improve your abilities.

The same is true for developing your personal and congregational leadership and outreach skills. You may never be recognized on the street as a mega-church pastor or make the Top Ten List of Fastest Growing Churches. However, you can make a greater missional impact on your community and improve your effectiveness in sharing the love of Jesus Christ with more people who need to hear and experience the life-changing message of the Gospel.

That's what this workbook is designed to do—help you improve your skills in eight related areas of mission and ministry.

What are the 8 Skills for Church Transformation?

The eight skills that you will develop as you walk through this workbook are directly connected to the eight hinge factors that result in church transformation. While there are tons of important leadership skills that are needed to lead a church effectively, these eight focus on the areas that actually open doors and turn churches around. In addition, these are eight skills that can be applied in any kind and size of a church. They are not based on the findings of the biggest churches, but on average-sized churches that have experienced transformation.

The first four skills are geared toward the pastor and other leaders in the church. The effectiveness of this skill development depends upon the full participation of the pastor of a local congregation. And it is preferable if the board and the primary leaders are also involved at some level. The final four skills focus on the entire congregation. Here are the eight skills:

Empowering God's People: The Pastor and other leaders spend significant time praying for, identifying, equipping, and supporting people in the congregation in order to release them for works of service in the community and the church.

Personal Leadership: Leaders demonstrate a commitment to their own physical, mental, spiritual, and relational needs and development. Great leadership begins with leading yourself well first.

Visionary Leadership: Leaders communicate the vision of a preferred future and a healthy sense of urgency about the direction and focus of the congregation.

Bridge-Building Leadership: Leaders dedicate some of their time (several hours per week) toward connecting the church to the community by assessing needs, meeting community leaders, and forming connections with unchurched and unreached people.

Community Outreach: The church has a strategy for reaching the community which results in building relationships that open hearts to the Word of Christ, sow the seeds of the Gospel and reap an eternal harvest.

Focused Prayer: The church develops a greater emphasis on prayer that incorporates intercession for those who need to know Christ.

Functional Board: The church has a governance structure that provides resources and support to the Pastor for the accomplishment of the mission and vision of the church, while also providing protection for the congregation through clear boundaries and accountability.

Inspiring Worship: The church has a worship service where the preaching, music, and atmosphere engage the culture with biblical and theological integrity.

How to use the Skill Builders:
The modules for the development of these eight skills can be processed in a variety of ways. They include:

1. Learning Community: The Skill Builder units are best used as learning modules for leaders in your church. Ask your leaders to work through the study on their own. Carve out time in your staff meeting, board meeting, retreat, or other training environment to answer the most pertinent reflection questions in small groups, fill out the personal assessment grid, and create an action plan to work on specific issues to empower others. Ensure that accountability partners are established to facilitate follow through with the action plans.

2. Self-study: Work through the study on your own. Carve out time to answer the most pertinent reflection questions, fill out the personal assessment grid, and create an action plan to work on specific issues to empower leaders.

3. Coach Assisted: While working through the study on your own, engage your coach to hold you accountable for action and follow through. Highlight a number of the reflection questions in each Skill

Builder and reflect on them with your coach to deepen your own level of awareness. Fill out the personal assessment grid, and create an action plan to work on specific issues and ask your coach to follow up with you regularly to review your progress.

4. "Buddy" Read: Work through the Skill Builder with another leader in your church or in your area. Carve out time to meet face-to-face to highlight a number of the reflection questions and to reflect on them with your "buddy" to deepen your own level of awareness. Fill out the personal assessment grid and create an action plan to work on specific issues and ask your "buddy" to follow up with you regularly to review your progress.

Hinge Factors Assessment

To enhance your experience with this Skill Builders manual, consider using the TCN Hinge Factors Assessment. Through participating in this assessment, you will receive insightful feedback on how your church members score your pastor and your congregation on the eight Hinge Factors, which are parallel to the eight Skill Builders.

Information is powerful, and our goal is to empower you and your congregation to reach your community with the Gospel. The Hinge Factors Assessment will help you understand your strengths and how to capitalize on them, while learning how to build up the areas where improvement is needed.

How it works: Your church members (minimum of 30, more for larger churches) will take a 10-15 minute on-line survey. Paper surveys are included as well. When the surveys are completed and the assessment is finished, you will receive a diagnostic report which will give you insights on how you are doing in each competency. (See the sample report in the Appendix.)

For rate information and to purchase the Hinge Factors Assessment, please go to the TCN website, www.transformingchurchesnetwork.org.

It is our hope and prayer that these Skill Builders will be valuable tools for you and your congregation as you strive to engage your community with the life-saving message of the Gospel of Jesus. May God swing open wide many doors for reaching lost people in your community as you grow in these eight vital skills!

1 Empowering God's People

Empowering people is *the* primary hinge that opens the door for maximum missional impact in the community. Without this powerful hinge in place, the leaders of the congregation will be weak or ineffective. All of the other tools in the box are directly linked to this pivotal factor, because the equipping and releasing of others for ministry is required for the effective implementation of the other seven factors. This is especially true in regard to the senior pastor. His ability to equip and empower others to engage in mission and ministry will often determine a church's ability to experience meaningful transformation.

The following exercises will equip the pastor and other key leaders to develop the skills needed to grow in this important ability to empower God's people for works of service.

10 Skills to Empowering God's People

#1: Praying

We are reminded to pray for workers for the harvest. God wants to use you to raise up and equip others, and it begins with a prayer focus. Consistently ask God to use you to mentor, coach, and develop others. Ask Him to give you mentoring eyes and to show you who has leadership potential in your congregation.

Reflection Questions:
- What hinders you from praying for God to raise up more proactive people in your midst?
- How often are you praying about empowerment? (rarely, occasionally, often)
- What steps can you take to find more time to pray for more people to engage in the work of God?
- Who can you be praying for more regularly?
   Names of current or possible people:

_____   _____

_____   _____

#2: Spotting

Look for faithful, available, and teachable people. Keep your eyes open for individuals who have potential or who are just waiting to be asked to jump into the game. Keep a list of individuals that you can be praying about who might have the willingness to take the risk and reach out to others.

Reflection Questions:
- What environments do you need to practice the skill of spotting in more regularly?
- How often do you practice the skill of spotting? (rarely, occasionally, often)
- What hinders you from spotting people with potential more regularly?
- Who have you spotted recently?
   Names of people you have identified recently:

_____   _____

_____   _____

#3: Exposing

Take someone with you when you are going to a meeting, extending care, making a visit, or attending training. Invite your friends and others to training opportunities that are offered at your church or at larger training events. Recruit as many people as possible to expose them to new ideas and fresh innovations that are being field tested in other churches. Another key exposure idea is to recommend books. Or consider doing a "buddy read" with your friends and debriefing it with them.

Reflection Questions:
- What exposure events or environments would you like to invite your friends or other people you know to?
- How often do you practice the skill of exposing? (rarely, occasionally, often)
- What ministry idea(s) would you like to expose your friends to?
- Who would you like to expose to some new ideas?
    Names of friends or others:

_____   _____

_____   _____

#4: Sponsoring

Many individuals need to be invited into leadership opportunities. Or they don't have the background or relationships to start an initiative. Use your position and influence with others in the church and in the community to open doors of opportunity by acting as a sponsor.

Reflection Questions:
- What existing ministry opportunities could you sponsor someone into?
- What new ministry opportunities could you sponsor someone into?
- What doors of opportunity could you open for others if you are bit more thoughtful and intentional?
- Who would you like to sponsor into ministry?
    Names of friends or others you would like to sponsor:

_____   _____

_____   _____

#5: Releasing
Often people need permission to try something new, to innovate, or to take a risk of some kind. Work on releasing by giving others an opportunity to run a whole meeting. Turn one whole night over to the group to plan and execute. Give a small assignment, something with which they will experience success. Gradually give more challenging assignments over time.

Reflection Questions:
- What are some ways that you could be more intentional about releasing others to try something new?
- Who needs my permission to take a risk?
- What existing meetings, groups, or ministries with which you currently work could you delegate small tasks or responsibilities?
- Who would you like to release in the future?
    Names of friends or others you will release:

_____   _____

_____   _____

#6: Debriefing
One of the best ways to empower others is to give appropriate feedback. People need to know what they have done well and help in knowing how they can improve. After a service, meeting, or ministry opportunity, sit down with your leader(s) and review what went well and what could be polished for the next time. Invite their input (raise their self-awareness) as you offer your input. You are simply trying to create an environment of learning and growth through the discipline of debriefing.

Reflection Questions:
- What times or settings are best for me to practice debriefing with others?
- What ministry would be benefit the most from debriefing with me?
- What makes debriefing a hard discipline for you?
- Who would you like to debrief with more regularly?
    Names of friends or others you will debrief:

_____   _____

_____   _____

#7: Supporting

The knack behind supporting is simply asking the question of a friend, "How can I help you," or "Do you need anything from me?" You want to instill the notion that you are a supportive net undergirding them. Often a friend will need assistance in trouble-shooting a ministry challenge or generating new ideas. Your availability can help them feel encouraged and on track. Stay supportive by floating around various ministries from time to time.

Reflection Questions:
- When would it be best to ask your friends if they need your help?
- What prevents you from being more supportive of your friends?
- Which friends may be stuck right now and would benefit from your support?
- Who needs your support?
    - Names of friends or others you will actively support:

_____   _____

_____   _____

#8: Modeling

You might have heard the phrase: "You watch, I do … You do, I watch." Modeling involves creating environments where others can learn to master something by watching you first. Your friends or others will want to know the "how's" and the "why's" as they watch you in ministry. Follow this up by giving them an opportunity for you to observe them in action and build in some time to debrief the experience with them.

Reflection Questions:
- What aspects of leadership would you like to model to others?
- What ministry opportunities are best suited for you to apply the "You watch, I do … You do, I watch" method?
- What aspects of ministry would you be best modeling to others?
- Who would you like to model ministry to and with?
    - Names of friends or others you would like to model for:

_____   _____

_____   _____

#9: Awareness Raising

Give the gift of clarity by asking lots of open-ended questions which enables someone to reflect on issues like, "How do you think the meeting could have gone better tonight?" or "What are a few ways that you think that you could improve as a discussion leader?" Rather than providing all of the answers, try using questions to help others figure out their next steps.

Reflection Questions:
- What kinds of environments could you practice awareness-raising in?
- What questions could you ask more regularly to raise awareness?
- Which ministry leaders would benefit the most from greater self-awareness?
- Who will you more intentionally raise awareness with?
    - Names of those you will try to raise awareness with:

_____   _____

_____   _____

#10: Coaching

Coaching is a more formalized relationship with an individual designed to help that person discover (know) and do the will of God through self-discovery guided by good questions. A coaching relationship is typically framed with the expectation of meeting regularly and focuses on helping someone move forward with goals and actions.

Reflection Questions:
- How many regular coaching relationships could you manage in my calendar if you met once a month with each person?
- Which ministry leaders would benefit the most from a coaching relationship?
- Which issues in our church could be addressed through a regular coaching relationship?
- Who will you initiate a regular coaching relationship with?
    - Names of potential leaders or existing leaders:

_____   _____

_____   _____

Self Assessment Grid

Instructions

Assess yourself in each of the keys to empowering God's people. If you are weak in an area or hardly practicing a key, shade in only a portion of the section. If you are practicing the key consistently then shade in all or most of the section. If you are practicing the key moderately then shade half of the section. Refer to the sample provided below to see how one leader assessed himself on the 10 Keys to Empowering God's people. Go to the next page to fill in your own grid.

Sample Assessment Grid

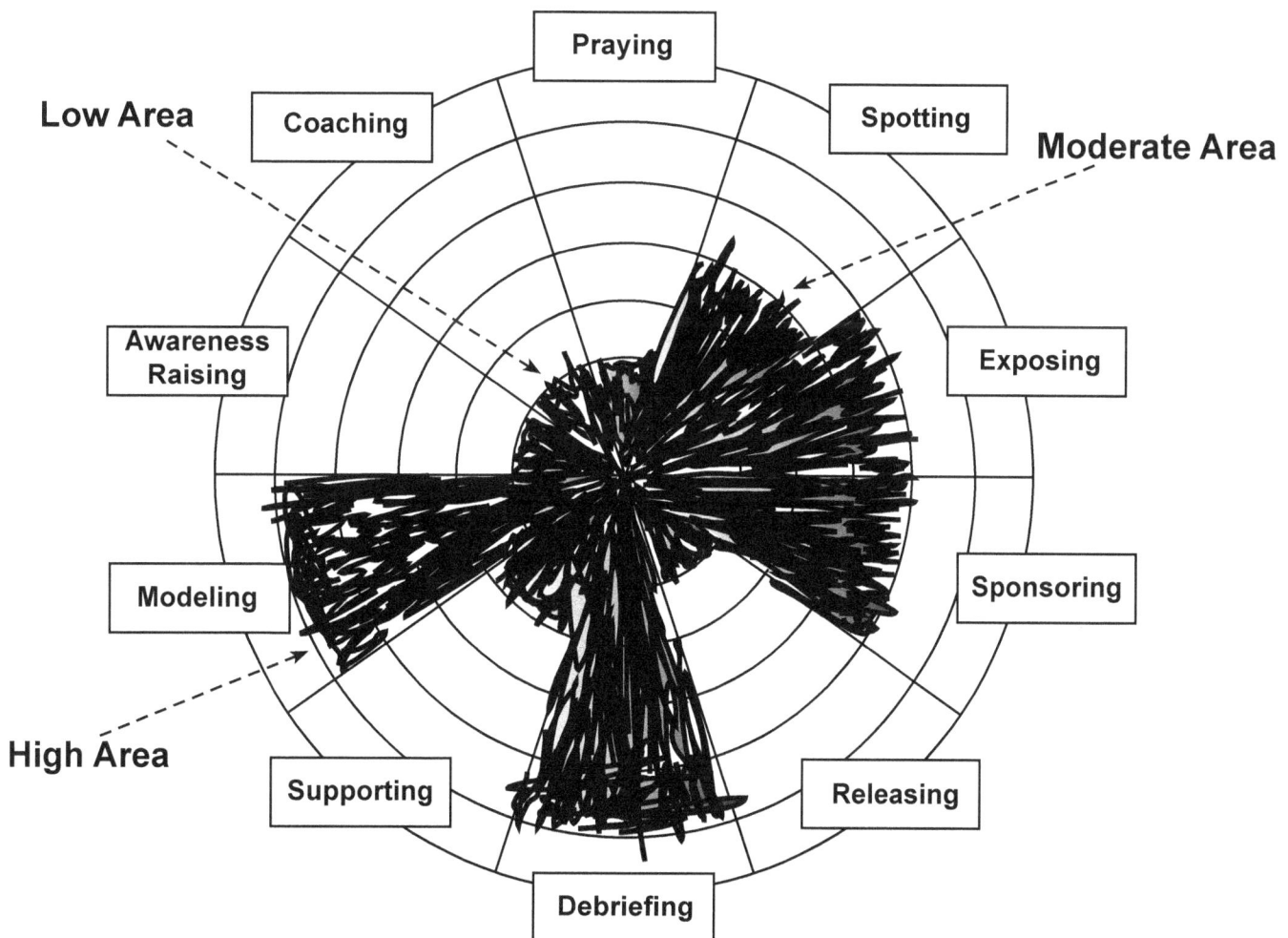

My Personal Assessment

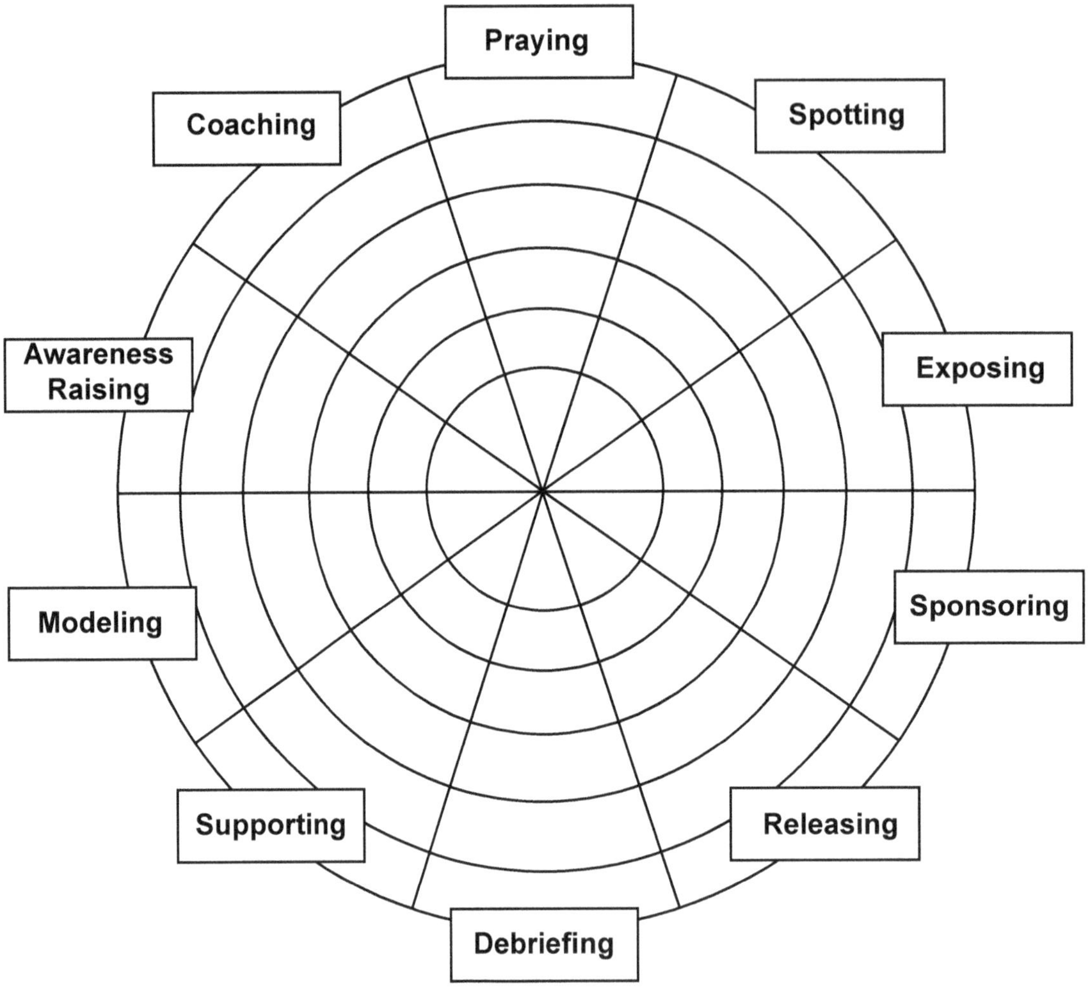
Praying
Spotting
Exposing
Sponsoring
Releasing
Debriefing
Supporting
Modeling
Awareness Raising
Coaching

Self Assessment Reflection Questions

1	How can I use my strengths to address some of my lowest scores?	
2	Which key, if practiced consistently, would enable me to be a more empowering leader?	
3	Who do I need to be more intentional with?	
4	What implications does this have for my use of time, my priorities, and what gets into my calendar?	

Empowerment Plan

Instructions: Use the worksheet below to list specific actions you intend to take related to this Skill Builder, the reflection questions and the self-assessment.

Specific Action	When & who will take this action?	Today's Status
1		
2		
3		
4		
5		
6		
7		
8		

2 Personal Leadership

How can leaders empower and guide the people of a congregation if they aren't able to demonstrate sound leadership in their own lives? Of course, the answer is that they can't; at least not very effectively. Leaders must be able to manage their own life well if they are going to lead others. They must embrace habits and disciplines that will help them live in a healthy and God-pleasing way, particularly in the areas of physical, mental, spiritual, and relational development.

These skill building exercises help leaders focus their energy and time so that they can invest in the right areas that will bring church transformation.

Personal Leadership Skills

Time Blocking:

Ministry and life are unpredictable. Yet, blocking out time in your calendar is critical to living an intentional lifestyle. Careful consideration needs to be given to issues related to the 6 P's (projects, priorities, planning, people, problems, and preparation) as you look at your up-coming calendar for the week. Setting aside blocks of time for these kinds of issues will help you create space for the important but "not urgent".

• When is the best time for you to set aside 30 minutes to time block the upcoming week on a regular basis?

• Which of the 6 P's do you need to create more space for?

On Time:

When we are working "in the ministry," we are hands-on in a variety of ways through meetings, services, appointments, and preparation. On Time is working "on the ministry" in a different use of time. It's when a leader has time dedicated to strengthening the ministry through planning, reflection, and learning. It's when you can slow down and set fresh direction, resolve a bottleneck, or create space to innovate.

• When is the best time of the week or month for you to create space in your calendar for On Time?

• What issues would you like to focus on during your On Time?

• Who will practice On Time with you to make it more productive?

Spiritual Disciplines:

Spiritual leaders need to lead from a well nourished soul. Leanness of soul can happen all too easily unless leaders finds spiritual rhythms that work for them. Every leader needs adequate space in daily life for solitude, reflection, prayer, and devotional Bible reading.

• When is the best time of the day for you have personal time with God?

• What usually gets in the way of your time with God?

• What changes would you like to make to reinvigorate your devotional life?

Fitness:

The fitness dimension ensures that we have the energy to live the life God is calling us to. Proper diet and exercise patterns become the "gift that keeps on giving" because of the inordinate benefits we experience. Taking care of our bodies is one of the highest leverage commitments a leader can make.

• What change do you need to make to increase the amount of energy you need?

• What do you need to stop doing or do less of to increase my energy?

• What do you need to do to increase the amount of exercise you am getting each week?

Zero Time:

Life and ministry has a way of filling up our "in box" as we roll through a typical week. Zero time represents a block of time dedicated each week to "getting back to zero." In particular, leaders need an opportunity to catch up on email, file papers, return phone calls, and clean up their desk. It's a reserved time in your weekly calendar when you get caught up and "clear the deck" for the weekend or upcoming week. Reserving zero time is psychologically freeing and allows you to get details off of your mind.

• When in your week could you position an hour or two of Zero Time?

• What kinds of details do you consistently get backlogged on?

Recovery:

Ministry is emotionally, spiritually, and physically exhausting at times. Leaders need adequate time in their week to replenish their reserves which have been depleted. Thoughtful leaders acknowledge the fact that ministry can swallow them up unless they build in adequate space for the recovery on physical, spiritual, and emotional energy. A "full" you is the best way to be a blessing to others on a consistent, long-term trajectory. Careful consideration needs to be given to your own self-care.

• What changes do you need to make regarding your day off that would assist you in your replenishment?

• What changes do you need to make in the amount of hours your are working each week?

• What one thing, done consistently, would help you stay "full" more of the time?

Personal Retreat:

God has invaluable treasures awaiting the leader who regularly withdraws from the battle front to replenish and refocus his life. Many leaders find that a monthly day-away has become the cornerstone of their effectiveness and vitality. Withdrawing has become for them the most important day of the month! A personal retreat is an opportunity to look at your life, look at your calendar, and look to God for wisdom and perspective. Fresh energy flows from being focused.

• Where and when could you begin experimenting with a half-day retreat format?

• What would you like the focus of your personal retreats to be?

• What changes would you need to make to enable you to take regular retreat days?

Learning:

Fresh input helps a leader to grow over a lifetime. A commitment to lifelong learning is one of the antidotes for overcoming personal plateau's. In today's climate, a leader has a number of outlets for learning including books, DVD's, podcasts, workshops, and conferences.

• What subjects or topics would you like to learn more about?

• What area of life or ministry do you need to learn more about?

• When is the best time of the week for you to dedicate time to learning?

Relationships:

Leading can be a lonely journey. Companions along the path make it safer and more enjoyable! Leaders are often giving and giving and find it difficult to find safe relationships where they can be authentic and vulnerable. And yet, having a few trusted individuals is critical for accountability and friendship.

• Who do you have in your life that is asking you the hard questions?

• What can you do to cultivate a few closer relationships?

• Who is someone that you would like to start building a new friendship with?

Coaching:

Leaders need developmental relationships from time to time from individuals who can sharpen and challenge them. Coaching positions another person to walk alongside a leader for support, accountability, and fresh thinking. Drift and plateau are all too easy. Reaching out and asking someone to coach us for a season of life can be one of the best ways to grow in our personal leadership.

• What one aspect of life or ministry could a coach help you with?

• What stands in the way of you finding a coach?

• Who would you like to ask to be your coach?

Self Assessment

Grid Instructions:

Self assess yourself in each of the dimensions of Personal Leadership.

- If you are weaker or hardly practicing a dimension of Personal Leadership, shade in only a portion of the section.
- If you are practicing the key consistently then shade in all or most of the section.
- If you practicing the key moderately then shade half of the section.

Refer to the sample provided below to see how one leader assessed himself on the 10 dimensions of Personal Leadership. Go to the next page to fill in your own grid.

Sample Assessment

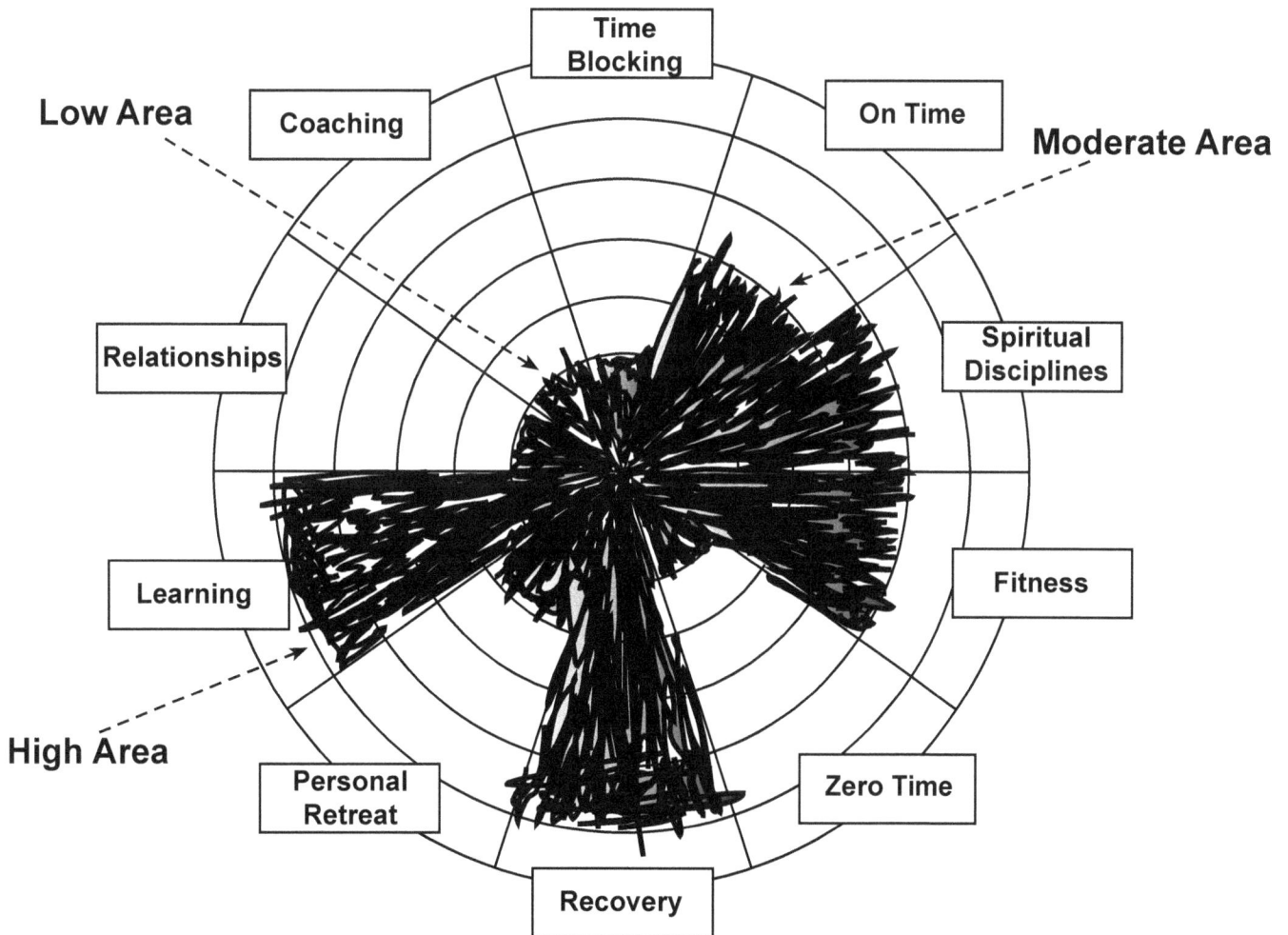

My Personal Assessment

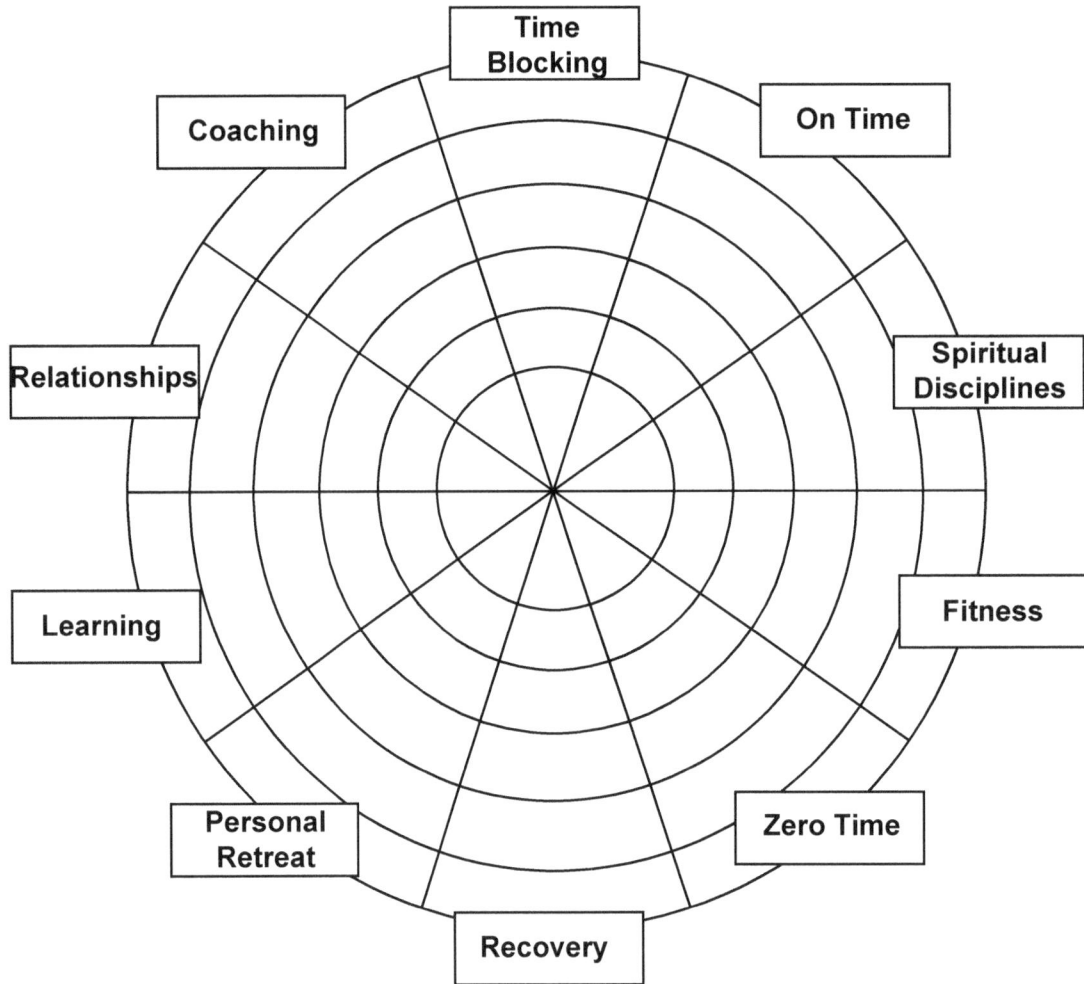

Time Blocking

On Time

Coaching

Spiritual Disciplines

Relationships

Fitness

Learning

Zero Time

Personal Retreat

Recovery

Self Assessment Reflection Questions

1	How can I use my strengths to address some of my lowest scores?	
2	Which key, if practiced consistently, would enable me to care for myself better?	
3	Who do I need to be more intentional with?	
4	What implications does this have for my use of time, my priorities, and what gets into my calendar?	

Personal Leadership Plan

Instructions: Use the worksheet below to list specific actions you intend to take related to this Skill Builder, the reflection questions and the self-assessment.

Specific Action Step	When will I take this action?
1	
2	
3	
4	
5	
6	
7	
8	

Visionary Leadership

Vision must be in the driver's seat as the church ventures out into the community. Vision—"a clear picture of a preferred future"—isn't discovered on a mountaintop or handed to most leaders engraved on tablets of stone. Rather, it comes by seeking the heart of God and seeing where He is already working in the community (John 5:16-20). However, discerning God's vision isn't even the hardest part of this task; communicating that vision is!

This skill builder is a bit different than the other seven in that it focuses on one specific skill that can be used in multiple settings and communication systems to cast an outward-focused vision and create urgency within the hearts and minds of God's people.

Key Visionary Leadership Skill: Stump Speech

When it comes to vision casting, the stump speech is a very simple, highly flexible communication tool. It is laser-like in its ability to communicate essential information. The discipline of crafting a stump speech will enable you to communicate vision in almost any setting. It is a powerful tool for reinforcing and anchoring a basic understanding of vision and direction. Put simply, stump speeches have three irreducible components. In addition, there are four basic principles that should be woven into all stump speeches.

Stump Speech Components:
- Component 1: Where are we headed?

- Component 2: How are we going to get there?

- Component 3: What part do I play?

Stump Speech Principles
- Principle #1: Tell stories

- Principle #2: Be positive

- Principle #3: Make it clear how they can participate!

- Principle #4: Communicate often and in a variety of settings.

Building Your Own Stump Speech

Instructions:
Read through the Stump Speech for the pastor of Light and Life Community Church below. Take note of how Pastor Jim has built his stump speech around the four words, Explore-Connect-Grow-Thrive. Watch for how he answers each component of a stump speech: (1) Where are we headed, (2) How are we going to get there, (3) What part I play. Also watch for the stories, his positive outlook, and how clear he makes it for people to see how they can participate.

After you have read through the stump speech example begin drafting your own with the Stump Speech Worksheets that have been provided at the end.

Stump Speech Example

Jim Parker's Stump Speech
Light and Life Community Church

Explore. Connect. Grow. Thrive

"We want to be a church that enables people to....
      Explore in homes
      Connect at church
      Grow in groups
      Thrive by serving

"Let me take a moment and share more about where we are headed with each of these four words: Explore, Connect, Grow, and Thrive. "

"We want to help people Explore their questions. On any given Sunday in our immediate community only 2 out of 10 adults regularly attends church. Chances are that 70-80% of the homes and apartments that surround Light and Life Community Church do not have a meaningful relationship with Christ. We need to be a church that changes those statistics. With that in mind, we will be starting a fantastic new course this coming fall called "Explore". "Explore" is a superb DVD curriculum that you would be proud to show to someone you know who has some spiritual questions or who isn't currently attending church anywhere. Just this week I talked with a pastor who has been running "Explore" in a few different homes. It was thrilling to hear about the people who are coming, the honest conversations that have been happening, and the hearts that are opening up to God. Here's the exciting part....we won't be running the "Explore" here at the church! We can't expect people in our community to come to us...we have to be willing to go them. We will be launching "Explore" in two homes which will be a more relaxed environment for spiritual conversations. Over the next few weeks, I would like you to consider two things related to this initiative:
      (1) Who do I know that I could invite to "Explore"?
      (2) Should I host "Explore" in my home?"

"We also want to be a church that makes it easy to Connect. I envision us being a church where meaningful friendships are formed. I want us to be a church that is passionate about our guests and newcomers. Research tells us that guests make up their mind about the friendliness of a church within the first five minutes. So people...first impressions are lasting impressions. Take Bob and Sue Smith. They recently told me that the main reason that they came back to Light and Life was because of the friendliness of Manny and Sandy Clark. The Clarks reached out to them during our worship service and even invited them to lunch that day. You might recognize that Bob and Sue were recently baptized ... thanks in part to the warmth of the Clarks. In the coming weeks and months you will notice a few changes on Sunday mornings. We are going to be thoughtful and intentional about this whole Connect piece. When you are on the church property we want to help build more and better connections between people. Remember though, these changes are for our guests primarily. You have a significant part to play in how well we connect with our guests! I am asking you to be much more thoughtful when you are here on Sundays and I want to ask you to go out of your way to get acquainted with someone new to the church each and every week. You can help this church be the friendliest church in town."

"I also said that I see us being a church where people Grow in their love for God. And God designed us to grow in community. In other words, we need the love and support of others around us. I was talking with Esther Quartez the other day and she couldn't stop raving about the people in her Monday night Growth Group. I was impressed when she said that the friendships she has experienced in her group have truly carried her through a very difficult season of work challenges. With this in mind, I want to invite you to join one of the three small groups that we will be starting this coming fall. All of us need a place where we can grapple with how to apply what we are learning to our own lives. Groups are a place where you can do the journey of life with others. If you are looking for a great way to kick-start your relationship with God or would like the chance to sink your roots even deeper then take the plunge this fall with one of our Growth Groups!"

"And finally, we want to be a church that helps people thrive. I envision people thriving at home, at school, at work, at the gym, on the athletic field, and even here at church. I see people who are learning the joy of giving their lives away. Light and Life Community Church must be a place where people experience the thrill of serving. For weeks we have wrestled with the unique needs of our community. Many of you have participated in our Community Survey and I am happy to report that the experience was enthralling. We had wonderful opportunities to talk with so many in our town and our eyes were opened to so many opportunities. After much consideration the leadership of the church has decided for this upcoming year to adopt our local elementary school. With the incredible budget cuts that have hit our schools in the last year we have formed a partnership with the administration at Hickory Elementary. So folks, our goal in the next year is to be an amazing blessing to the school in any way that we can. Teachers are short on supplies, students are desperate for after school tutoring, families are struggling to send their kids to school with adequate food, computers are needed for the classrooms. I could go on and on … We want the teachers and families of Hickory to feel loved by their local church this coming year. I wish you could have been in the principal's office when I met with him last week to finalize some of the plans. His eyes teared up when he said the following: "Jim, I want you to know that your generous offer to assist Hickory in the next year has been a true shot in my arm. You have no idea how excited we are by the possibilities." In the coming weeks you will be hearing more about the Hickory Project and I want to invite you to thrive by giving your life away!"

"So there it is friends…it is indeed an exciting future that God is leading us toward. Remember we want to be a church that helps people: Explore. Connect. Grow. Thrive.

Build Your Own Stump Speech

Step One:
Find a few simple words that capture the essence of what you and your church need to focus on. Use the space below to tinker and test some phrases that may work for you in your setting. In the example provided the simple words were: Explore, Connect, Grow, Thrive. Here are a few other examples from other churches:

Example #1: Learn, Relate, Serve

Example #2: Win, Build, Send

Example #3: Transform, Mature, Impact

Example #4: Build, Bring, Belong, Become, Bless

My Stump Speech "Simple Words" (i.e. Explore, Connect, Grow, Thrive)

Step Two: Place your first stump speech word in the blank space in the left side of the table below (in box A, B, C). Then move to the far right side of the table and draft some thoughts about how you would answer the questions in the middle. After you have completed this table move on to the other tables that have been provided to help you flesh out your stump speech for your other Stump Speech words.

My First Stump Speech Word	Stump Speech Component	Things I'd like to say in the stump speech ...
A. (i.e. Explore)	Where are we heading?	
B. (i.e. Explore)	How are we getting there?	
C. (i.e. Explore)	How can others participate?	

My Second Stump Speech Word	Stump Speech Component	Things I'd like to say in the stump speech ...
A. (i.e. Connect)	Where are we heading?	
B. (i.e. Connect)	How are we getting there?	
C. (i.e. Connect)	How can others participate?	

My Third Stump Speech Word	Stump Speech Component	Things I'd like to say in the stump speech ...
A. (i.e. Grow)	Where are we heading?	
B. (i.e. Grow)	How are we getting there?	
C. (i.e. Grow)	How can others participate?	

My Fourth Stump Speech Word	Stump Speech Component	Things I'd like to say in the stump speech ...
A. (i.e. Thrive)	Where are we heading?	
B. (i.e. Thrive)	How are we getting there?	
C. (i.e. Thrive)	How can others participate?	

Step 3:
Give your stump speech. Begin testing the speech out in conversations, small group settings, meetings, and eventually in a sermon. Have someone from outside the church (another pastor or your coach) to give you feedback on how to polish your stump speech into an even more compelling message.

4 Bridge-Building Leadership

In order to open doors to the community, it is crucial for the church's key leaders to get out of the office and engage the community. For many church professionals and volunteer leaders who are accustomed to leading from the office or the board room, this can be scary and intimidating. Yet, there is no better way to learn about the needs, the culture, and the people in a local community than by actually meeting with them and talking to them. This hinge is all about the pastor and other key leaders modeling for the congregation how to connect the church to the community by assessing needs, building bridges, meeting people, and forming connections. Through this modeling process, leaders gain credibility as they invite the congregation to go along with them in building relationships with and serving the needs of the lost and unreached people in their own neighborhoods.

These skill builders will equip leaders to do what they want to see happening in the rest of the church. If the pastor and other key leaders don't learn these things, then equipping the rest for them will be an uphill battle.

Bridge-Building Skills

Prayer
In all of the ministry demands that come with leadership, praying about outreach related concerns helps evangelism stay on your heart. Ask the Lord to: (1) Give you a sense of burden for your community, (2) Provide open doors to share the love of God with others, (3) Help you to model a heart for evangelism to your congregation, (4) Move in the hearts of those you are trying to reach.

• When is the best time in your day to integrate a prayer focus for your own personal bridge-building opportunities?

• What bridge-building opportunities do you want to focus your prayer energy on in the coming month?

Busyness
Many leaders simply do not have the time for bridge building because they have too much going on. You may have to eliminate something from your life to free up time. Develop the discipline of putting bridge-building time into your weekly calendar.

• Which activities or commitments do you need to let go of to free up time for bridge building in the community?

• When is the ideal time in your week to carve out space for bridge building?

Expectations of Others

Ministry comes with expectations … some are voiced and others are not. Many believe that "their" needs should be met and take priority over other ministry concerns. Many leaders do not feel released by their congregations to spend time in the community. Building bridges is not "what we hired you for" is a common reframe. Leading your church toward an external focus will mean that you help others see why you are building bridges and why it's a critical part of your ministry.

• How will you communicate with the congregation about "why" you are spending several hours a week bridge-building?

• What (group or person) do you need to gain permission or agreement from regarding bridge-building time?

Extroversion

Getting out of the office and into the community requires a leader to take the initiative. Building bridges requires phone calls, making appointments, and meeting with people. For those who are more introverted, bridge building will be a stretch out your comfort zone.

• What will help you to get the ball rolling in bridge building?

• If you are more of an introvert, what steps can you take this month to force yourself out of your "comfort zone."

Accountability

All of us lose heart from time to time. An accountability partner who is asking you about your bridge-building efforts is a strategic choice. Your partner can ask questions like: "How many lost people are you praying for?", "How many intentional relationships do you have that you are prayerfully wanting to share the gospel?", "When was the last time you shared the gospel?", and "Who have you recently built a bridge with in the community?"

• Who could be an accountability partner for you in your bridge-building efforts?

• What specific questions would you most appreciate accountability for?

Distraction

Outreach into the community often gets squeezed out of a leader's life because it stops being a priority. There are so many needs and issues that need attention in the life of the congregation that leaders find it difficult to get out into the community. The distractions of the church can make it challenging to stay passionate about evangelism.

• What distractions in your life and ministry are making it difficult for you to stay focused and concerned about building bridges?

• What practical step or steps can you take in the next month to address these distractions?

Calling

Many leaders express confusion regarding their calling and outreach. The key question that is often unresolved is: "Do I need to take primary responsibility for leading our congregation into the mission field in our community?" There is a dynamic tension between shepherding and bridge-building or between "inreach" and "outreach." Leaders must be clear about where building bridges fits into their understanding of their call.

• How does building bridges in the community fit into your understanding of your call?

• What ramifications would "taking primary responsibility for leading your church into the mission field" have for your ministry priorities.

Awareness

Many leaders are surprised by how much they don't know about their community and the specific needs that are present. Studying, interacting, questioning, and assessing are all necessary disciplines in "spying out the land." Interacting with schools, social service agencies, and local government organizations will provide invaluable data as you try to determine specific ways that you can invest in the community.

• Which offices or organizations would you like to sit down with in the near future to assess needs in the community?

• Which community leaders do you need to get an appointment with?

• What issues are you particularly interested in learning more about?

Creativity

Building bridges into the community requires a measure of creativity and possibility thinking. Being curious about what God is up to in your community will open many options for bridge building. Give yourself permission to tinker, experiment, and even pilot some fresh thinking or approaches for reaching out into the community. Learn from what other churches are doing in your community and beyond.

• If you knew that you could not fail, what bridge into the community would you like to build?

• What are some steps that you could take in the next month to move toward that idea, dream, or calling from God?

Redirecting

There is a strong likelihood that there are a number of relationships and organizations that you are already in contact with that could assist you in building bridges. Redirecting or re-thinking how you interact with these contacts may open up fresh possibilities for you.

• Which existing relationships (individuals or organizations) could you be more intentional with in the future?

• What would it mean specifically for you to redirect or rethink how you approach these relationships?

Self Assessment

Grid Instructions:

Self assess how well you are managing each of the dimensions of Bridge Building.

- If you are stalled due to little progress or if the dimension needs considerable attention then shade in only a small portion of the section.
- If you are managing the dimensions consistently well then shade in all or most of the section.
- If you are managing the dimension moderately (needs improvement) then shade half of the section.

Refer to the sample provided below to see how one leader assessed himself on the 10 dimensions of Bridge Building. Go to the next page to fill in your own grid.

Sample Assessment Grid

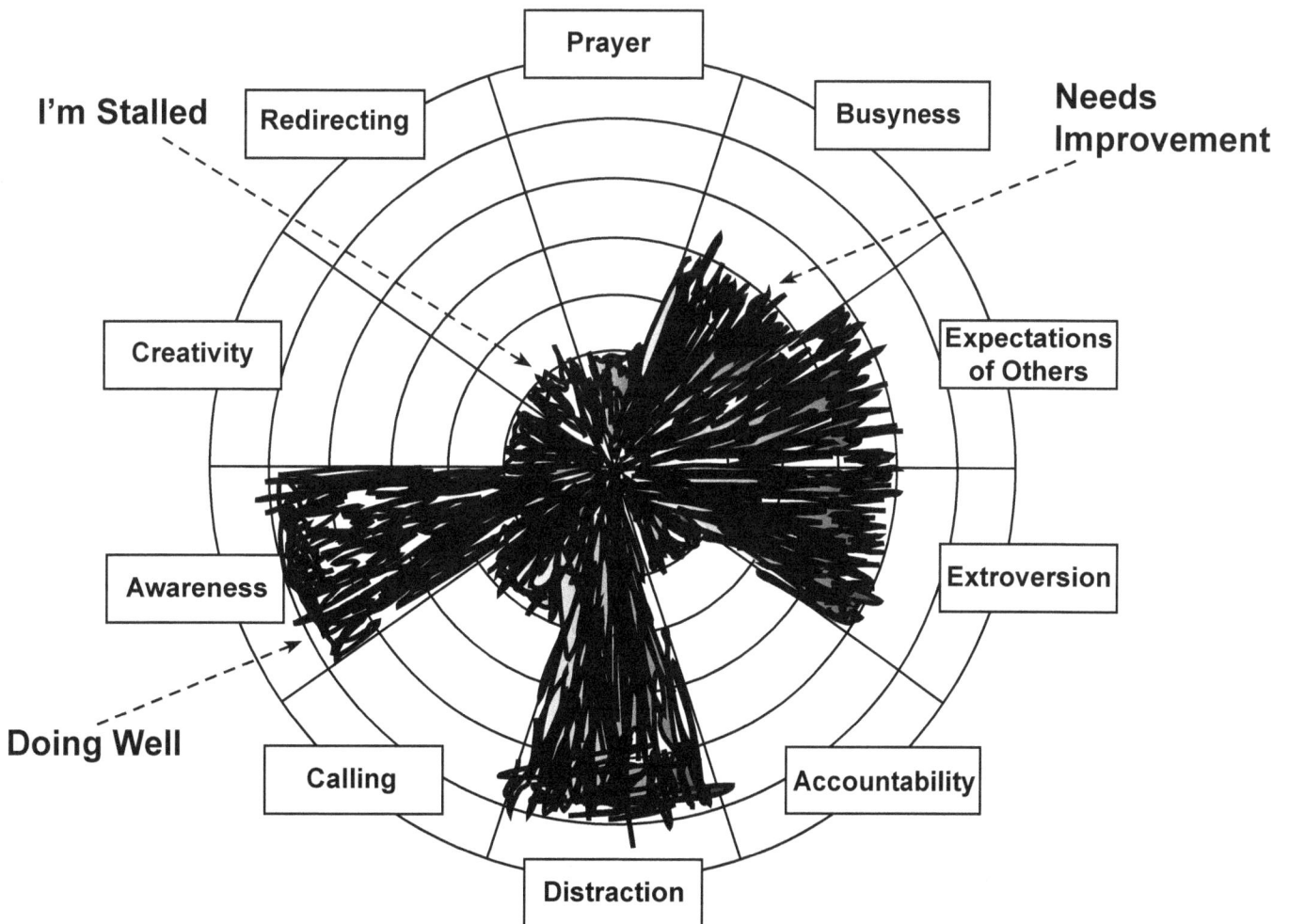

My Personal Assessment

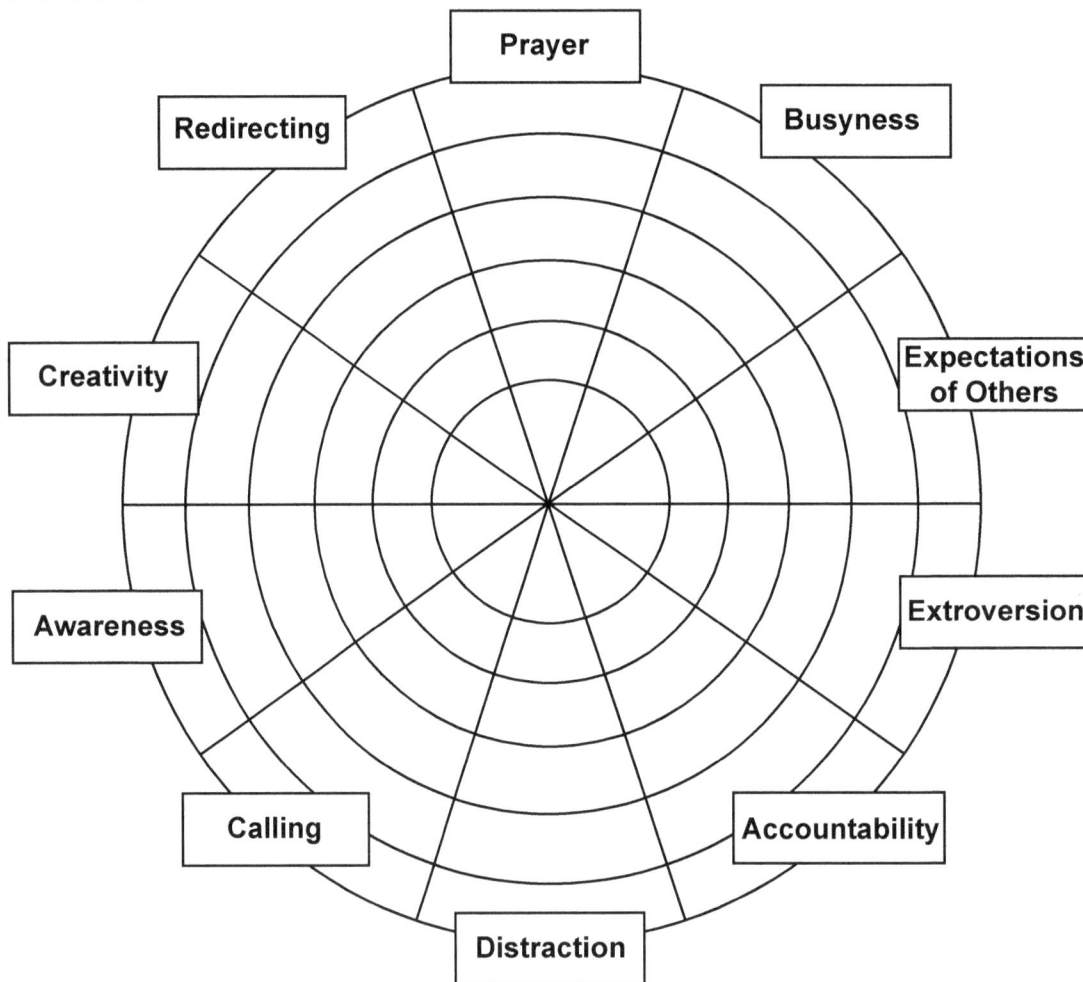

Prayer

Redirecting

Busyness

Creativity

Expectations of Others

Awareness

Extroversion

Calling

Accountability

Distraction

Self Assessment Reflection Questions

1	How can I use my strengths to address some of my lowest scores?	
2	Which key, if practiced consistently, would enable me to be a more bridge-building leader?	
3	Who do I need to be more intentional with?	
4	What implications does this have for my use of time, my priorities, and what gets into my calendar?	

Bridge-Building Plan

Instructions: Use the worksheet below to list specific actions you intend to take related to this Skill Builder, the reflection questions and the self-assessment.

Specific Action Step	When will I take this action?
1	
2	
3	
4	
5	
6	
7	
8	

5 Community Outreach

This powerful hinge swings the door of the church open for God's people to become incarnational disciple makers. Jesus said to His first disciples, "I will make you fishers of men" (Mark 1:17). Today, He might say to us, "You have to go fishing to catch a fish!" Serving people opens their hearts to new relationships and the Word of Christ. The church is not limited to a piece of property and a building. The scattered church lives, works and plays in a specific piece and place of Americana. Whether it is the inner city or suburbia or some place in between, there we are. Where we find ourselves is the context in which we can demonstrate the love of Christ, build relationships that open hearts to the Word of Christ, sow the seeds of the Gospel and reap an eternal harvest. This is community outreach and has been since the days that Christ walked the streets of Jerusalem, and it works!

Leaders can use these skill building exercises to develop a process that will equip people to do just that. It will result in a strategy and plan that will naturally lead to opening even more doors for community outreach.

Introduction

Skills for Reaching Your Next 50

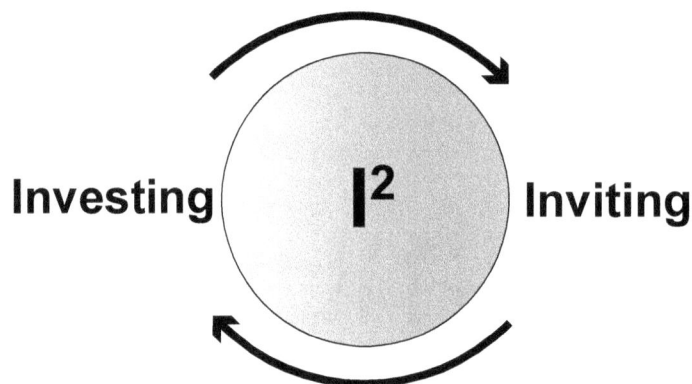

Investing I^2 Inviting

The reality is your church knows The Next 50 people that will become a part of your faith community. The Next 50 live next door, roam our office complexes, teach in our children's schools, and play tennis on the weekends in our parks. The I^2 strategy is a simple to understand way to find, attract, and include The Next 50 people that God wants to be a part of your church family.

The I^2 strategy is built on the powerful principle that the people of your congregation are already in relationship with The Next 50. You don't have to go to elaborate, sophisticated, or complicating lengths to win over The Next 50. Rather, it's a matter of teaching a simple concept to the church and consistently reinforcing it throughout the year.

This Skill Builder is constructed around two words: Invest and Invite. The intention of this learning piece is to help you think through your approach to investing and inviting The Next 50 in your community. We recommend that you take the long view with the I^2 strategy. This is really more about reinforcing a way of life than it is about running a program. With this in mind, please consider developing an I^2 Team or an Outreach Team that will help shoulder the load for advancing this strategy.

4 Keys for Investing in The Next 50

Key #1: Prayer

Prayer is plowing the ground. Praying for our Next 50 is a strategic activity as we align ourselves with what God is already doing in the Harvest Field. Research has born the truth that praying by name for people we know that need the love of God in their lives is extremely effective. Many churches use prayer cards or prayer bookmarks to remind people to consistently make spiritual investments in The Next 50 relationships that they have. Others have found that Prayer Walking in their community is an effective way to ask for God's favor and power to be released.

Key #2: Hospitality

Our homes are a lighthouse. Food is the great equalizer because all of us have to eat and it doesn't require that much more energy to cook for a few more. Asking people into our homes for a meal, dessert, or coffee can be a great way to invest in a relationship. Parties are another wonderful opportunity for inviting friends into a home, whether it's based around a holiday or a special occasion.

Key #3: Fun

What do popcorn, a tennis racquet, a pizza, and a big screen TV have in common? The common denominator is fun. Everyone needs more fun in their lives and having fun with others is a hugely popular way to invest in relationships with people who need God. Whether it's going to the movies, eating sushi at a local restaurant, watching the big game on TV, or sipping a beverage at your local coffee shop, investing in fun with others is a "no-brainer."

Key #4: Invite

The key to the Invest and Invite strategy is built on people being intentional about inviting friends, neighbors, and work associates to church sponsored events or opportunities. People in the congregation must be thinking ahead about the next service or event that the church is sponsoring that they want to invite others to. You already know The Next 50 people who are going to join your church. Most of them will find their way to your church because someone invited them.

4 Keys for Inviting
The Next 50

Key #1: Promotion

Promotion is a multi-faceted dimension of the Invest and Invite strategy. Today, an up-to-date website has become the equivalent of the yellow pages and makes it easy for people in the community to know what is going on in your church. Secondly, simple invitational pieces need to be developed (business cards, tickets, fliers, etc.) so that potential guests can be handed an invitation for worship services or a large event that is upcoming. Lastly, Sunday Services are a fantastic way to remind the congregation about upcoming outreach opportunities and to encourage them to extend invitations.

Key #2: Sunday Services

There are two aspects of maximizing the invitational power of your Sunday Service. The first is to re-think the "guest experience" of your Sunday morning service. How would a guest feel in your service? Is there anything that can be done to make your first-time guests more at home? Secondly, anchor points through the year need to be maximized. Christmas and Easter are still the top religious holidays that The Next 50 will come to without much hesitation. The church must invite them though.

Key #3: Special Events

Assuming that you have conducted some kind of community survey, you should be armed with solid data on felt needs in your area. For example, if you have decided to focus on young families you could hold a parenting workshop or a marriage enrichment seminar that The Next 50 could be invited to. In addition, the calendar year has a number of special events sprinkled through the year that could easily be turned into an outreach opportunity. For starters, consider an event that is themed around any of the following: July 4th, Halloween, New Years, Valentine's Day, and the Super Bowl. Lastly, consider a service project in your community that The Next 50 would be willing to help out with. The Next 50 would love to help clean a park, tutor at a school, or coach a sports team.

Key #4: Next Steps

All of the Investing and Inviting needs to lead The Next 50 to another step. In other words, special events and your weekend services should never be "the end." The critical question that must be planned for is, "What is the next step that we can provide for our guests?" It could be a new sermon series, or a new small group on parenting, or a service opportunity in the community. As you plan your outreach event calendar for the year make sure that you give adequate attention to what happens "after the event" so that your guests come back and take the next step closer to becoming a part of Your Next 50.

I² Review

Instructions: Before moving on to the church assessment, capture some of your thoughts, questions, and ideas from the 4 keys to Investing and 4 keys to Inviting.

Keys	Ideas and Reflections
Invest	
Invite	

Church Assessment

Grid Instructions:

Assess how well the church is managing each of the keys for Community Outreach.

- If your church as a whole is stalled due to little progress or if the dimension needs considerable attention then shade in only a small portion of the section.

- If your church is managing the key consistently well then shade in all or most of the section.

- If your church is managing the key moderately (needs improvement) then shade half of the section.

Refer to the sample provided below to see how one church assessed itself on the 8 keys of Community Outreach. Go to the next page to fill in your own grid.

Sample Assessment Grid for a Church

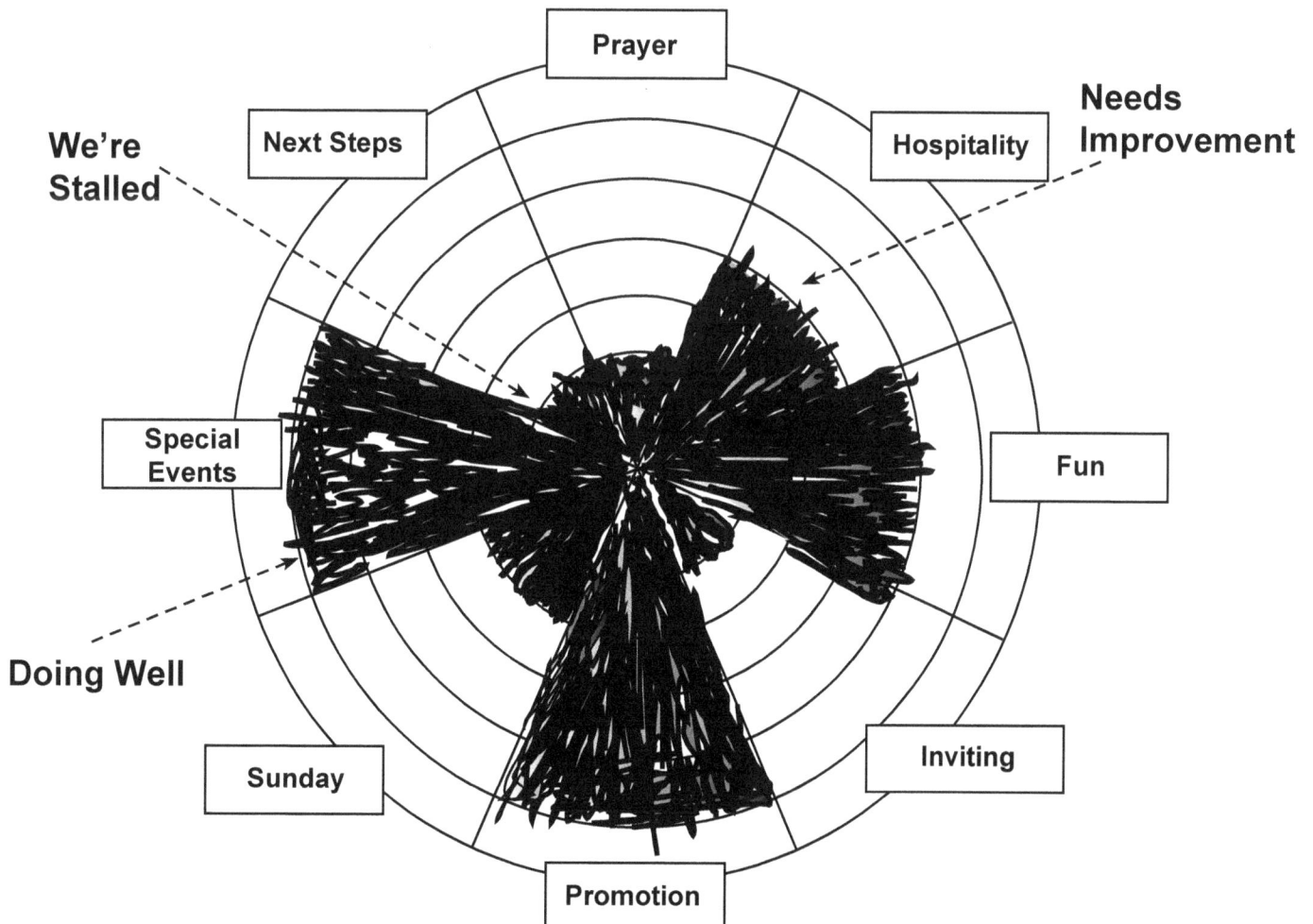

Our Church Assessment

- If your church as a whole is stalled due to little progress or if the dimension needs considerable attention then shade in only a small portion of the section.

- If your church is managing the key consistently well then shade in all or most of the section.

- If your church is managing the key moderately (needs improvement) then shade half of the section.

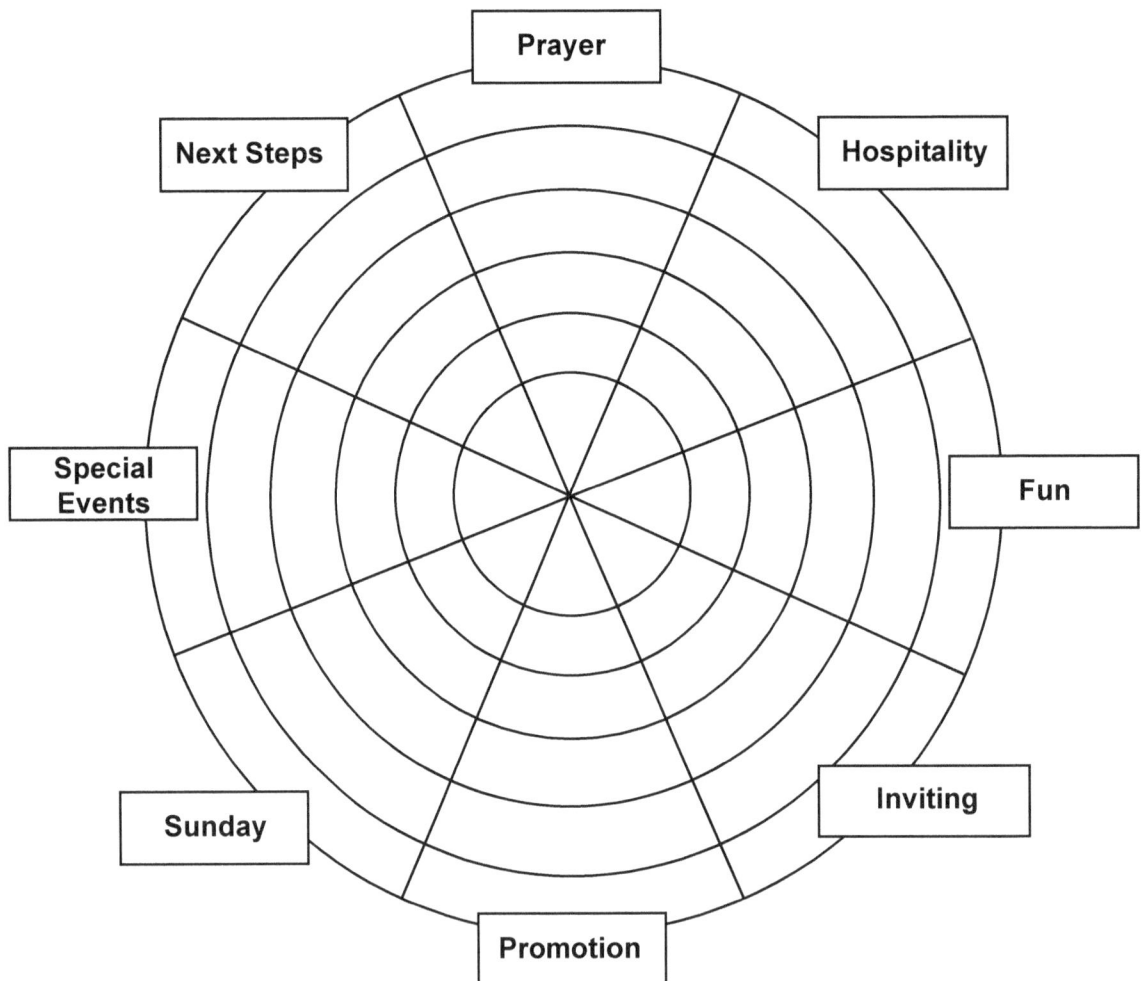

Church Assessment Reflection Questions

1	What can we do to mobilize prayer in our congregation for The Next 50?	
2	How can we encourage our church to practice hospitality with people that they already know who need the love of God?	
3	What are the best ways for our church family to have fun that The Next 50 would also enjoy?	
4	How can we strengthen and mobilize our church to be more intentional about inviting others to church services and special events?	
5	What are some ways that we can improve the promotion of events so that our people find it easier to invite others?	
6	Which Sunday services in the coming year should we maximize and intentionally promote amongst our people so that they will invite The Next 50?	
7	Which special events in the coming year should we build and promote as safe places for our church family to bring The Next 50?	
8	What Next Steps pieces do we need to develop to ensure that our Next 50 come back?	

Community Outreach Plan

Instructions: Use the worksheet below to list specific actions you intend to take related to this Skill Builder, the reflection questions and the assessment.

	Specific Action Step	When will we take this action?
1		
2		
3		
4		
5		
6		
7		
8		

Annual Outreach Planning Chart

	Jan	Feb	Mar	Apr	May	June	July	Aug	Sept	Oct	Nov	Dec
Sunday Services												
Outreach Events												

Outreach Event Planner

Instructions: Reproduce the chart below and brainstorm action steps that you will need to work through to plan an Outreach Event or a special Church Service. Every event needs its own stand-alone planner. Use the questions below to stimulate your thinking. One action step goes on one Post-it Note™. Don't worry about sequencing the notes initially. You can do that after you have brainstormed.

Next Step Questions:
> Who should be included in this?
> When can we get started?
> What needs to sorted out first?
> What could get in the way?
> How will we get started?
> How should we promote this?
> What decisions need to get made?
> When will we review our progress?
> Other Questions? _____

30-Day Action Steps	60-Day Action Steps	90-Day Action Steps

Place Post-it Notes on the Next Steps Chart

6 Focused Prayer

Focused prayer is an emphasis on prayer that incorporates intercession for those who need to know Christ. There are a number of dimensions related to this goal and cannot be accomplished by the pastor or
leaders alone. St. Augustine once said, "Pray as though everything depended on God. Work as though everything depended on you." Prayer
for the lost and unchurched by name and prayer for the church's vision
to become reality cannot be overlooked. Prayer during the times of
worship, in prayer groups, during board and staff meetings and in pri-
vate devotions will have impact. As Saint. Paul says, "Pray continually"
(1 Thessalonians 5:17).

This skill builder works best as a team-building experience with those
who exercise leadership in the church and with individuals who could
help mobilize the type of prayer explained above.

Introduction

Focused Prayer Skills

Pastor's Prayer Life:

Focused prayer begins with the prayer life of the pastor. The congregation looks to the pastor to model a heart for God and authenticity regarding his own personal habits regarding prayer. Congregations who take prayer seriously have pastors who lead by integrating a prayer emphasis in as many aspects of church life as possible. Regular practice of spiritual disciplines by the pastor positions him to lead by example and to demonstrate spiritual vitality.

• How would you currently rate the vitality of the pastor's prayer life on a scale of 1-10 (10 is high)? Why?

• What steps could be taken in the next two months to strengthen the pastor's prayer life? What obstacles might you encounter?

Worship Service:

A worship service provides a natural opportunity on a weekly basis to integrate training, modeling and encouragement to the congregation regarding focused prayer. In particular, up-front prayer during a worship service that emphasizes and spotlights the needs of those who need Christ reminds a congregation to focus outwards. Most lay people need to hear and see how others pray before they feel confident to pray themselves.

• How could prayer for the lost and for your church's harvest field be more intentionally integrated into various elements of your worship service?

• What creative ideas could you experiment with in the worship to highlight the importance of prayer?

Prayer Coordinator:

Many churches find that appointing a "champion" of prayer helps a church sustain momentum with intercession. Mobilizing and supporting an individual who can bring leadership and energy on a consistent basis will ensure that prayer efforts stay on the front burner. Creative energy will be released when a prayer coordinator owns the responsibility to stir a heart for prayer in the congregation. Typically, this individual would raise up an "intercession team" who would help shoulder the task.

• Who comes to mind when you think of a "prayer coordinator" role in your church?

• What resources (books, dvd's, workshops) inside and outside your denomination should a prayer coordinator be exposed to which would equip them in mobilizing prayer?

Small Group Emphasis

Sunday school classes and small groups is a natural place where focused prayer should be regularly integrated. Class and group leaders need to be reminded to install time for prayer during every gathering. Everyone that attends knows someone who needs the love of Christ and gatherings are unique opportunities to remember these people in prayer. These informal and smaller meeting times are a fantastic place to help people feel more confident in the "how to's" of prayer.

• What could be done in the next three months to equip class and group leaders with ways to integrate harvest field praying into their gathering times?

Training:

New ideas and approaches related to prayer is one of the best ways to grow congregational prayer strength. Books, workshops, DVD's, and podcasts can open up a church to fresh and exciting possibilities. In a world where innovation is the norm, new streams of input will keep your congregational prayer energy consistently vibrant.

• What would be the best way to offer some training in prayer within the next three months?

• Which book, CD, DVD, podcast, or Webcast would you like to expose the church to?

Devotional Resources:

Many find it helpful to put some measure of structure around their prayer lives. Structure enables an individual to stay focused, to not lose one's train of thought, and to be thoughtful about interceding on a number of fronts. Some have found prayer cards, which list a number of categories and prompters, to be extremely beneficial. Find a few resources that will work for your congregation and will stimulate prayer lives and be committed to staying with them for at least a year.

• Where can you go to find a few devotional resources that will stimulate your church to pray more regularly?

• What is the best way to consistently promote these resources so that the most amount of people will begin using them?

Sermons:

Throughout a calendar year, there are a number of sermon passages that lend themselves toward greater instruction on prayer. Look for every opportunity to highlight the power of prayer when preaching. In particular, many are looking for practical ideas that will help them be more consistent in prayer. Preaching that offers suggestions, illustrations, and personal stories related to praying for those who need Christ will inspire and motivate others to action.

• How can your preaching integrate a greater emphasis on the power of prayer?

• What personal stories and practical advice about praying for the harvest field can you share with others in the next three months ?

Prayer Gatherings:

Praying with other people is one of the quickest ways to turbo charge congregational prayer energy. When thinking about creative ways to mobilize prayer, some emphasis should be given toward launching opportunities for people to pray together. The expressed purpose of these gatherings needs to be focused on the vision and mission of the church, along with real people in the community who need Christ.

• Who could help lead or facilitate prayer gatherings for the church?

• When would be the most logical time of the week to pilot a prayer gathering?

• What specific issues and needs in the harvest field do you want to focus on?

Prayer Model

Many are stumped by the notion of praying for the hearts and minds of friends and neighbors who need the love of Christ. Some instruction on how to pray and even categories to pray will help an individual's reluctance to pray. For starters, we can pray:

- Pray that the person's heart be prepared, so that it will be "good soil" for the seed (Mk. 4:8),
- Pray that Satan will not be able to steal the seeds of truth (see Mk. 4:15,)
- Pray that the Word becomes revelation through the lifting of the veil (2 Cor. 4:3,4),
- Pray that the root of pride in them be broken (2 Cor. 10:3-5),
- Pray that the person come to true repentance (2 Pet. 3:9).

- In what environments could you teach people a simple model for praying for the harvest field?

- What other ways could you teach people to pray evangelistically for the community?

Modeling:

Prayer is both taught and caught. One of the most effective ways to mobilize more focused prayer is to be intentional about modeling it across the life of the church. Meetings can start and end with extended times of prayer. Worship services demonstrate how to address God in prayer. Small groups and ministry teams can devote a portion of their gathering times to pray. More will pray when they are encouraged, taught, and inspired by those who have developed "prayer muscles."

- What can we practically do to model prayer more effectively across the life of the church?

- What can we do to raise up more leaders who will model prayer for others?

Assessment Grid

Instructions:

Individually assess the church related to Focused Prayer in each of the dimensions covered in this skill builder (and then compare with others if appropriate).

- If the church is weaker or hardly practicing a dimension of Focused Prayer, shade in only a portion of the section.
- If the church evidences the dimension consistently then shade in all or most of the section.
- If the church is moderate then shade half of the section.

Refer to the sample provided below to see how one church assessed itself on the 10 dimensions of Focused Prayer. Go to the next page to fill in your own assessment grid. Once each person has filled in the assessment, average the scores for each dimension and create a "Church Profile" around the average scores. The reflection questions and the plan can be done as a group exercise after the "Church Profile" has been created.

Sample Focused Prayer Assessment Grid

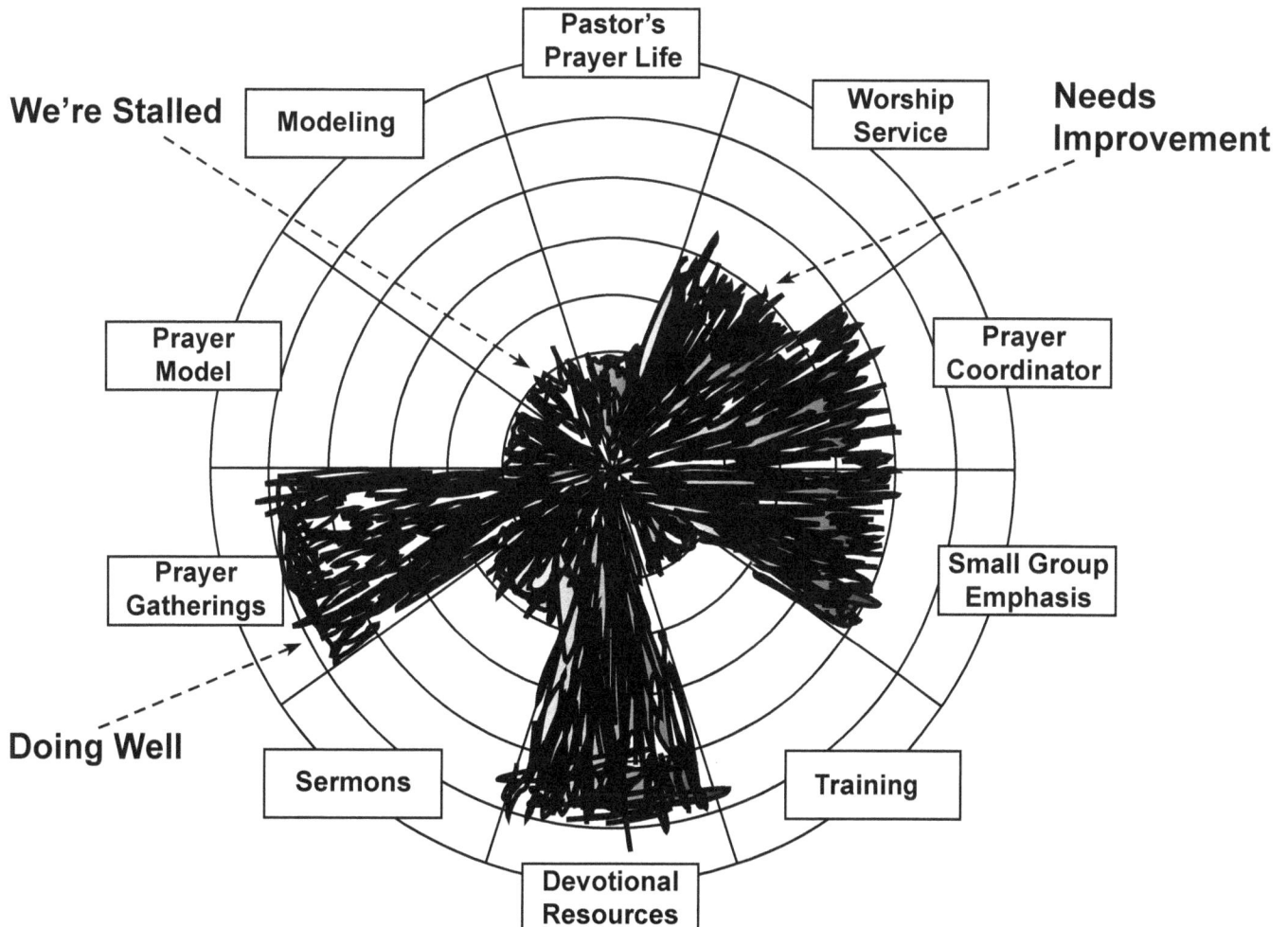

My Assessment of our Focused Prayer

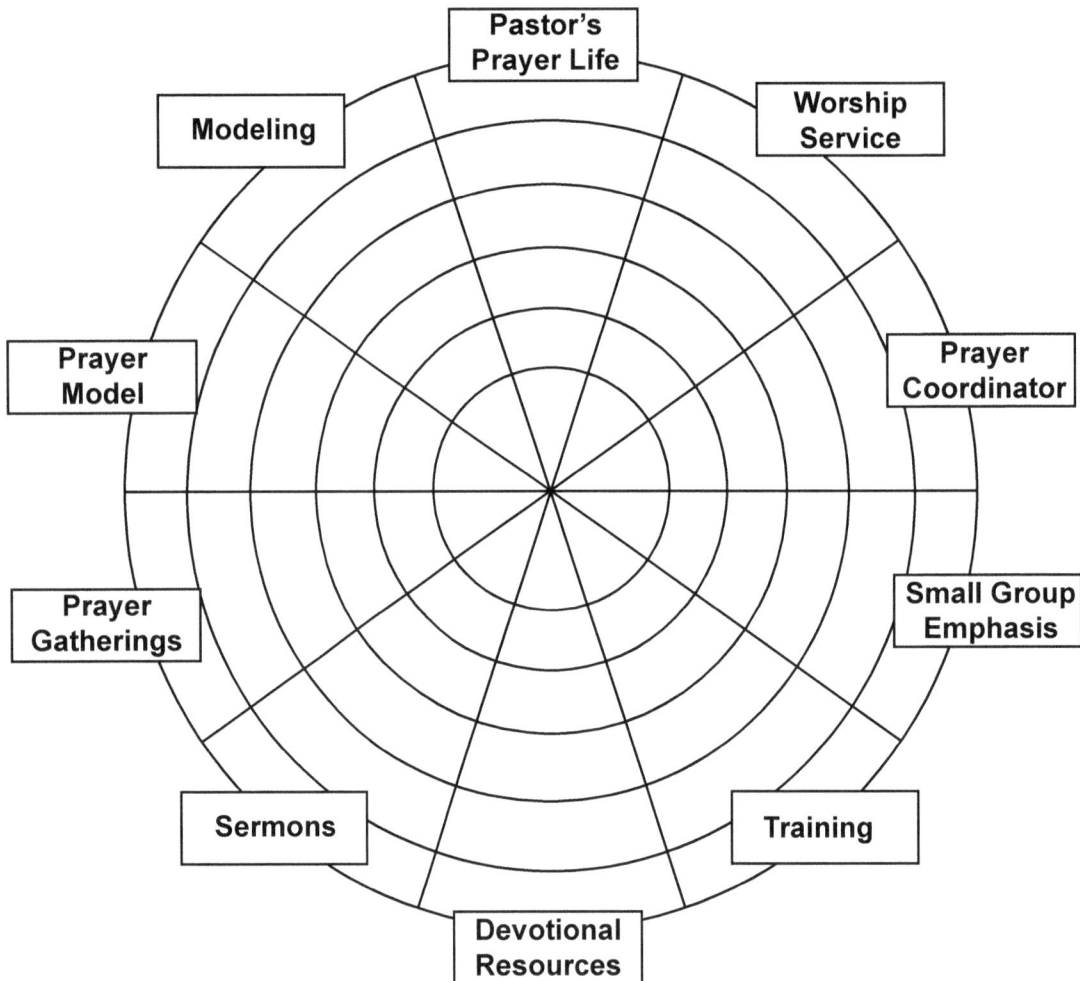

Assessment Reflection Questions

1	How can we use our strengths to address some of our lowest scores?	
2	Which key, if practiced consistently, would enable us to have more focused prayer?	
3	What issue(s) need to be addressed first to enable us to have more focused prayer?	
4	What implications does this have for our use of time, priorities, and future planning?	

Focused Prayer Plan

Instructions: Use the worksheet below to list specific actions you intend to take related to this Skill Builder, the reflection questions and the self-assessment.

	Specific Action Step	When will we take this action?
1		
2		
3		
4		
5		
6		
7		
8		

7 Functional Board

Our research revealed that church boards are vital to the transformational process. This can be done in a variety of models as there are a number of governance structures and approaches that have proven to work well. While not subscribing to any one model of governance, a healthy and robust board is immensely valuable for a pastor and a congregation. For a board to consistently function well, it must balance two dynamic components (1) Attend to the spiritual needs of a congregation (matters of "being"), and (2) Review and bring meaningful accountability to the management of the ministry (matters related to "doing"). Functional Boards must support the Pastor's leadership role while providing protection for the congregation through boundary principles. The board makes sure that the Pastor has all the resources and support that are needed in order to accomplish the mission and ministry of the church. In turn, the Pastor is held accountable for the vision of the church. The application of these broad principles is congregationally specific and must be contextualized by the stakeholders of the church for transformation to occur.

Effective boards take time and effort to develop. This skill builder is designed to be a tool that a Pastor should use with his board to kick-start discussions about opportunities for improvement as a governing board.

Functional Board Skills

The Board's Role:
It is not uncommon for the members of a church board to be unclear about the role of a board. Confusion abounds related to decision-making, goal-setting, congregational needs, follow-through, and board meeting agendas. When there is lack of clarity about the role and purpose of a board, meetings often become problem-solving sessions. This could be an opportune time to revisit the board's role in your congregation. Find a book that the board could study together and carve out dedicated time to putting some declarations down on paper.

• From your perspective, what is the role of the board?

• What needs to be clarified amongst board members to enable the group to function more effectively?

Courage:
Shepherding a congregation takes courage. The ability for board members to speak honestly to one another is essential. When a board finds itself in a position where there is very little healthy disagreement, problems are bound to occur. Differing perspectives ensure that solid decisions are made and prevent a board from becoming too comfortable. In addition, assessing next steps and addressing core health issues requires a board to confront reality.

• What would stimulate greater levels of honesty and healthy disagreement in our board meetings?

• What next step or congregational health issue will require the board to lead courageously?

Relationships:

Over time a board can become a very task-oriented environment. To counteract this, many boards dedicate portions of a meeting or entire meetings to enhancing the relational rapport of its members. Relational warmth amongst a board fosters higher levels of trust and honesty which impacts effectiveness.

• What has the board done in the last two months to cultivate stronger relationships with one another?

• What fresh approaches could the board try in the next six months to enhance relationships?

Spiritual emphasis:

Again, the tasks and challenges of shepherding a congregation can hinder the amount of time a board gives to grow spiritually together. However, effective boards don't rush past the need to pray together and to study God's Word with one another. Time should be allotted to pray over decisions, direction, challenges, and needs related to the congregation.

• What steps can the board take to ensure that extended times of prayer are integrated into board meetings?

• What resource could be used to enhance the spiritual maturity of the board (a book, Bible study, or DVD resource)?

Learning and Development:

Boards that function well together are ones that consistently develop themselves. Board development may not happen at every board meeting but carving out time to read a book or watch a DVD on a "hot topic" helps ensure that a board's capacity is expanding.

• What particular issues or opportunities are facing our congregation in the next 6-12 months?

• What board issues (i.e. decision making, goal setting, conflict) could be strengthened through learning?

• What books could we read that would truly expand our board's leadership capacity?

Ministry Direction:

Functional boards have a good grasp on two issues related to ministry direction: (1) Where are we headed, and (2) How are we going to get there? Many boards find it helpful to use a SMART Goal format. When writing your goals, the following checkpoints are essential:

S = Specific (Goals must not be vague. They must be direct and specific.)
M = Measurable (How will we know the goal has been accomplished?)
A = Attainable (Goals must be achievable given reasonable effort and focus.)
R = Realistic (Do we have the financial and people resources to accomplish this?)
T = Time bound (When will the goal be accomplished?)

• When will the board carve out time to set a few SMART goals for the church?

• What one or two things must the church accomplish to be healthier in the next year?

Development of the Pastor:

Effective boards recognize that pastors are in a very demanding profession. It is all too easy for a board to run past the fact that a pastor deserves to be supported and encouraged. Annual reviews give a board an opportunity to assess the health and effectiveness of the pastor. Additionally, a board is the one place where a pastor is to be held accountable for personal and professional goals.

• How effective is your current review process of the pastor and how can it be improved in the future?

• How well is the board ensuring that the pastor set personal and professional goals? How can this be improved?

Board Leadership Hats:

Boards that function effectively ensure that three leadership hats are relating well to one another (the pastor, the chairperson, and the secretary). Most agree that someone other than the pastor should be the chairperson for the board. The working relationship of the chairperson and the pastor is critical to set meeting agendas and to ensure that solid follow through is sustained from one meeting to the next. Secondly, the secretary plays a critical role in capturing detailed notes regarding discussions and decisions that have been made at meetings. These must be circulated to all board members shortly after a meeting is concluded.

• What can be done to strengthen the working relationship of the chairperson and the pastor?

• How could you improve the way that ideas, discussions, and decisions get captured during meetings?

Focused meetings

Healthy, effective boards run focused meetings. A well run, productive meeting takes fore-thought and planning by the pastor and the chairperson. Agendas are framed ahead of time around the answers to questions like: (1) What is important for us to discuss at the upcoming meeting?, (2) What decision do we need to make?, (3) What must we follow up on from a previous meeting? and, (4) How much time should we allot to each agenda item?

• What will enable the board to run more focused meetings in the future?

• How can the chairperson and pastor work more closely together to frame meeting agendas?

Written Guidelines:

Functional boards commit themselves to documenting guidelines related to (1) Board responsibilities and expectations, (2) How the board stewards the personal and professional life of the pastor, (3) Appropriate legal, financial, and moral boundary lines that will help protect the ministry of the church.

• What written guidelines for the board are missing or need to updated?

• Which resource will we use to help us frame better written guidelines (Examples include *Structure Your Church for Mission* by Kurt Bickel and Les Stroh [www.strobickan.com] and *Winning on Purpose* by John Edmund Kaiser)?

Assessment Grid

Instructions:
Self assess the Board in each of the dimensions covered in this skill builder.
- If the board is weaker or hardly practicing a dimension of a Functional Board, shade in only a portion of the section.
- If the board is practicing the key consistently then shade in all or most of the section.
- If the board is practicing the key moderately then shade half of the section.

Refer to the sample provided below to see how one board assessed itself on the 10 dimensions of being a Functional Board. Go to the next page to fill in your own board assessment grid. Once each board member has filled in the assessment, average the scores for each dimension and create a "Board Profile" around the average scores. The reflection questions and the plan can be done as a group exercise after the "Board Profile" has been created.

Sample Board Assessment Grid

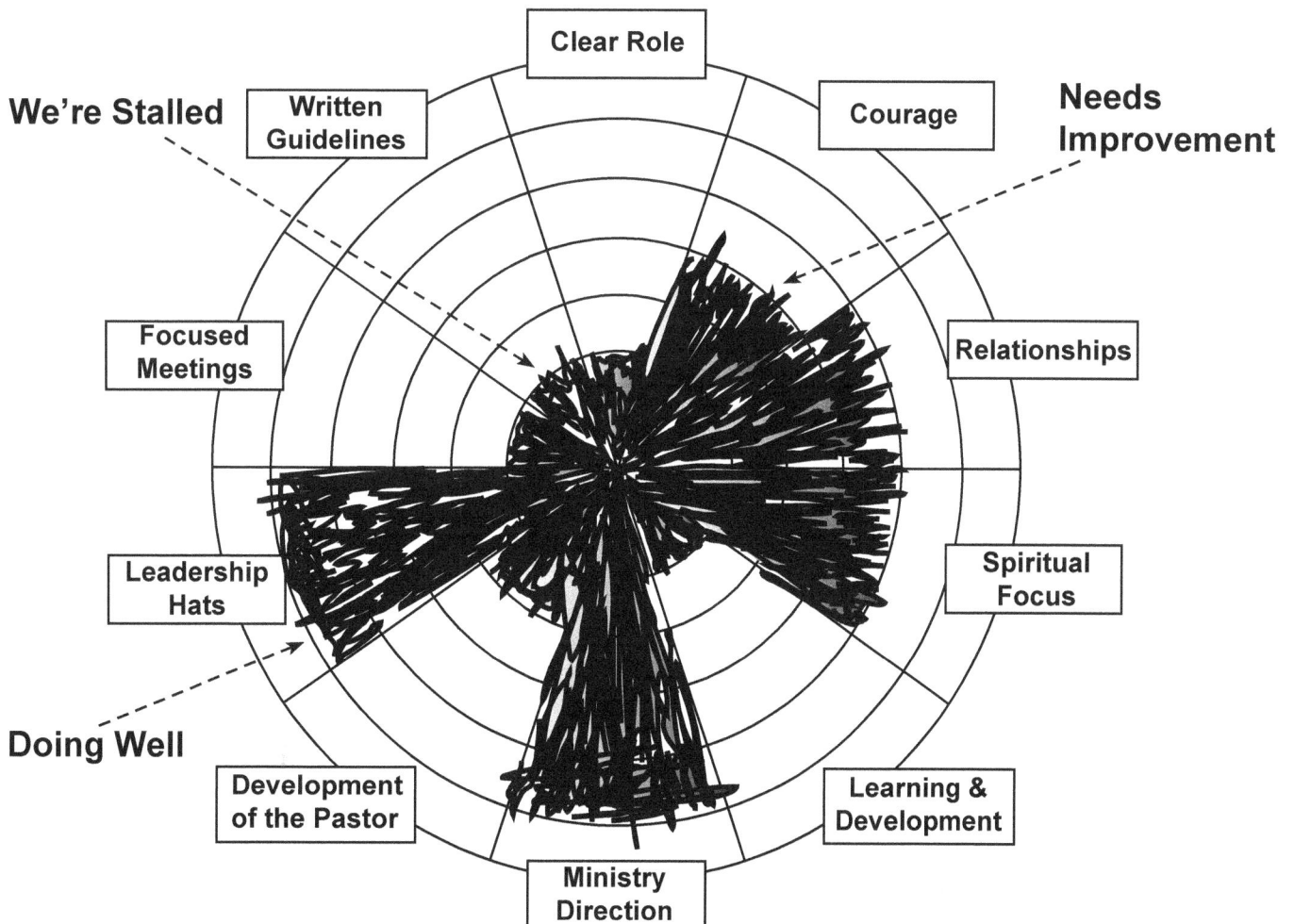

My Assessment of Our Board

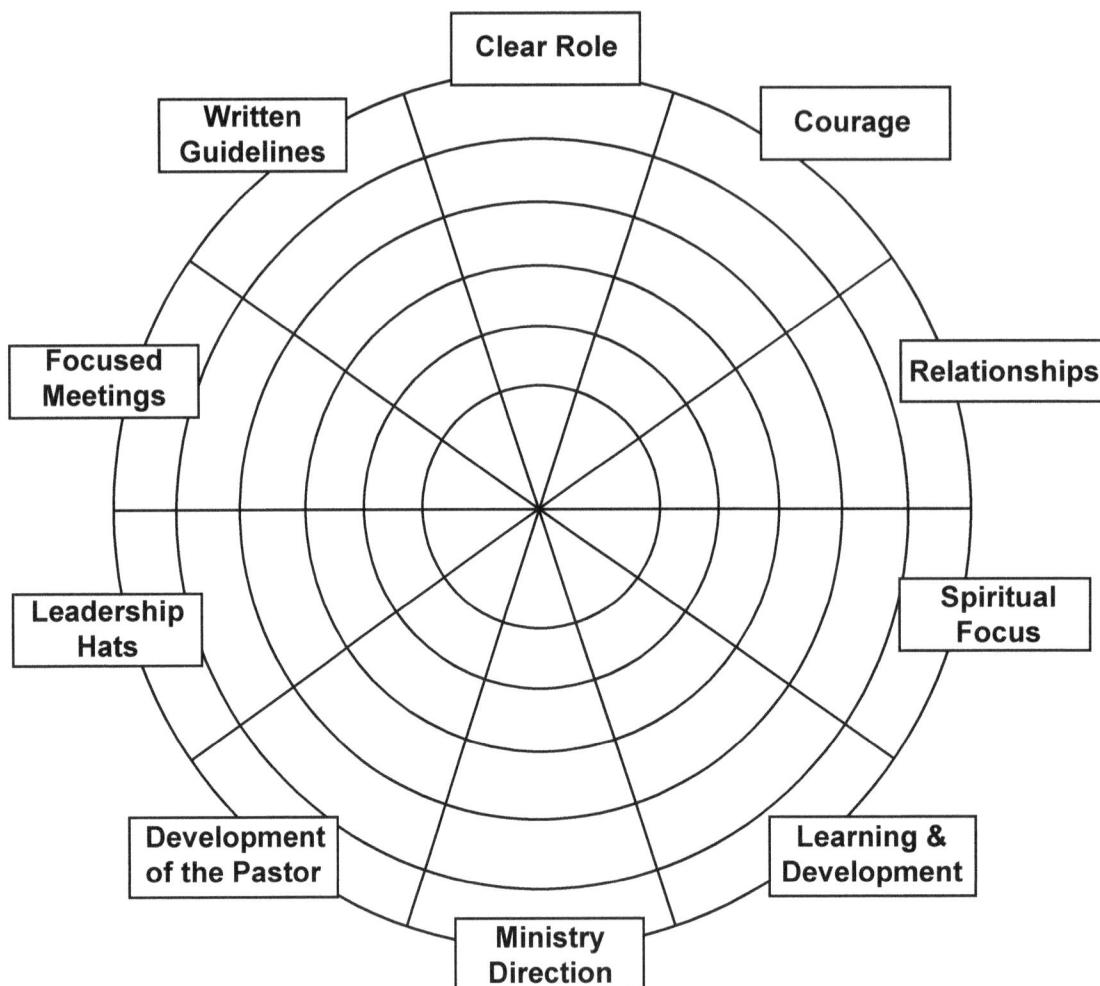

Clear Role

Written Guidelines

Courage

Focused Meetings

Relationships

Leadership Hats

Spiritual Focus

Development of the Pastor

Learning & Development

Ministry Direction

Assessment Reflection Questions

1	How can we use our strengths to address some of our lowest scores?	
2	Which key, if practiced consistently, would enable us to have a more functional board?	
3	What issue(s) need to be addressed first to enable us to function better as a board?	
4	What implications does this have for my use of time, our priorities, and what gets into our board calendar?	

Functional Board Plan

Instructions: Use the worksheet below to list specific actions you intend to take related to this Skill Builder, the reflection questions and the self-assessment.

Specific Action Step	When will we take this action?
1	
2	
3	
4	
5	
6	
7	
8	

8 Inspiring Worship

Seekers attend church hoping to make friends and connect with God in a way that is meaningful to them. Mature believers are often looking to go "deeper" in their knowledge and experience of a personal, yet sovereign Lord and Savior. There is no "one size fits all" worship experience. Both formal and informal worship may provide a way for a wide variety of people to sense the presence of God. Passionate and professional, enthusiastic and contemplative, historical and contextual, or challenging and comforting are all poles on a wide spectrum of approaches that may facilitate individuals in experiencing God's presence in a time of worship.

Inspiring worship services need to be experiences where the preaching, music, and atmosphere appeals to a growing number of people from the community. There are a number of dimensions related to this goal and cannot be accomplished by the pastor or Worship Leader alone. With this in mind, TCN strongly encourages that this skill builder ultimately be done as a team-building experience with those who could become a Worship Team or a Worship Planning Team.

Inspiring Worship Skills

Team Approach:

The creation of worship services that attract people from your community takes energy and thoughtfulness. It's highly unlikely that a quality worship service can be executed week in and week out without a team to help shoulder the burden. A weekly or biweekly team environment is the perfect place to consistently give emphasis to planning, evaluation, innovation, and learning.

• How would you currently rate the effectiveness of your Worship Team on a scale of 1-10 (10 is high)? Why?

• What steps could you take in the next two months to strengthen or form a Worship Team? What obstacles might you encounter?

Creative Planning:

Worship services which inspire attenders will be more creative with forethought. A regular team meeting is a stimulating time to wrestle with questions like: (1) How can the music support the "big idea" of the sermon? (2) What can we do to be welcoming to guests? (3) What future ideas do we have to enable the congregation to truly focus on the Lord during our worship services?

• What creative ideas would you like to try in the next six months?

• What idea or ideas, if implemented, would improve the effectiveness of your worship service planning?

Openness to Innovation:

Consistently inspiring worship services will necessitate being exposed to new ideas and approaches. Consider sending volunteers to visit churches in your area from time to time (within your denomination and outside it!). Study a book together like *Can't Wait for Sunday* by J. Michael Watters or *Worship Matters* by Bob Kauflin and implement the best practice ideas that you think will work in your setting. The internet is a valuable resource for training and innovations which are cost effective and can be viewed together as a team.

• What will you do in the next three months to expose yourself (and team) to fresh thinking about worship services?

• What churches do you need to visit in the next year?

Relevant Preaching:

Feedback from trusted voices in the congregation is an effective way to keep preaching relevant. Sermon evaluation positions a pastor to assess his style, content, and overall communication effectiveness. It's wise for sermons to be evaluated weekly or biweekly with a simple tool that gives the pastor feedback on accessible and helpful his sermon was. Also, it is prudent to measure the pulse of the congregation from time through a survey to uncover the most significant real-life issues people are wrestling with.

• Who could help evaluate the preaching and what feedback should the pastor receive related to the sermon?

• What real life issues need to be addressed more consistently during sermons?

Guest Care:

Warm and welcoming churches encourage guests to return again and again. Viewing your worship service and church campus through the eyes of a guest helps you address blind spots that could hinder the experience of your visitors. Dimensions of guest care that could be valuable to consider would include: adequate signage, friendliness of children's workers, ushers and greeters, relational warmth of regular attenders, the first impression look and feel of your campus, and the visitor follow-up system.

• Currently, what "first impressions" would a guest have of your church?

• What area can you proactively strengthen to improve the quality of care your guests experience?

Participatory:

Inspiring worship services engage and involve people so that they are participating rather than spectating. Singing, readings, prayer, and silence are all maximized to stir people's hearts and move participants toward greater connection with God.

• How can participants be challenged to engage more fully during the Worship Service?

• Which aspect of your service needs a greater level of participation (reading, singing, prayer, silence, or the sermon)? What enhancements can be made to address this?

Visual:
Integrating visual components into a worship service is helpful in a few ways. We remember what we see much more than what we simply hear. Preaching that encompasses the more visual, right side of the brain with stories, objects, and pictures will cement greater learning and recall. Secondly, the use of creative slide presentations truly enhance participants ability to focus on God.

• How can your preaching be more visual by using right brain communication methods?

• What are ways to incorporate more visual components before, during, and after your worship services?

Appropriate Amplification:
The advent of amplifiers in the last century has forever altered the contemporary worship service. The critical question that must be addressed by the Worship Team and the congregation is, What is the appropriate level of volume for those who attend the service? And more importantly, how do our guests feel about our volume? Is it too quiet for them, just right, or too loud? In addition, are your audio and visual systems adequate or do they get in the way of the worship experience because of sound distortions and glitches?

• What is the appropriate amount of amplification for the people you are trying to reach in your community?

• What audio or visual system upgrades need to be made in the near future to enhance your Worship Services?

Song Selection

Most congregations would be wise to make a declaration regarding their philosophy regarding the songs that they sing. Are you striving to be traditional, contemporary, or blended in your song selection? How accessible would a guest find the songs that you sing? So much inspiring worship music is being generated all over the world. Congregations are enriched by exposure to new songs and styles, albeit at an appropriate pace of introduction.

• How would a guest from your community feel about the songs that you typically sing?

• How can the Worship Team expose itself and the congregation to the inspiring music of the last decade?

Next Generation:

Worship methods change over time and the wise church allows the upcoming generation to find its own authentic worship expressions. Tastes in songs, instruments, and creativity can be extremely diverse from one generation to the next. Inspiring worship services need to give a voice to the next generation of church leaders and worshippers. Younger volunteers need to be recruited on to the Worship Team and should also be included in planning meetings.

• Which younger leaders need to be included in future worship service planning?

• How can you be more proactive in involving the next generation in worship service leading and participation?

Assessment Grid

Instructions:

Individually assess (and then compare with your Worship Team) the worship services in each of the dimensions covered in this skill builder.

- If the worship services are weaker or hardly practicing a dimension of Inspiring Worship, shade in only a portion of the section.
- If the worship services evidence the dimension consistently then shade in all or most of the section.
- If the worship services are moderate then shade half of the section.

Refer to the sample provided below to see how one church assessed itself on the 10 dimensions of being Inspiring Worship. Go to the next page to fill in your own assessment grid. Once each person has filled in the assessment, average the scores for each dimension and create a "Church Profile" around the average scores. The reflection questions and the plan can be done as a group exercise after the "Church Profile" has been created.

Sample Inspiring Worship Assessment Grid

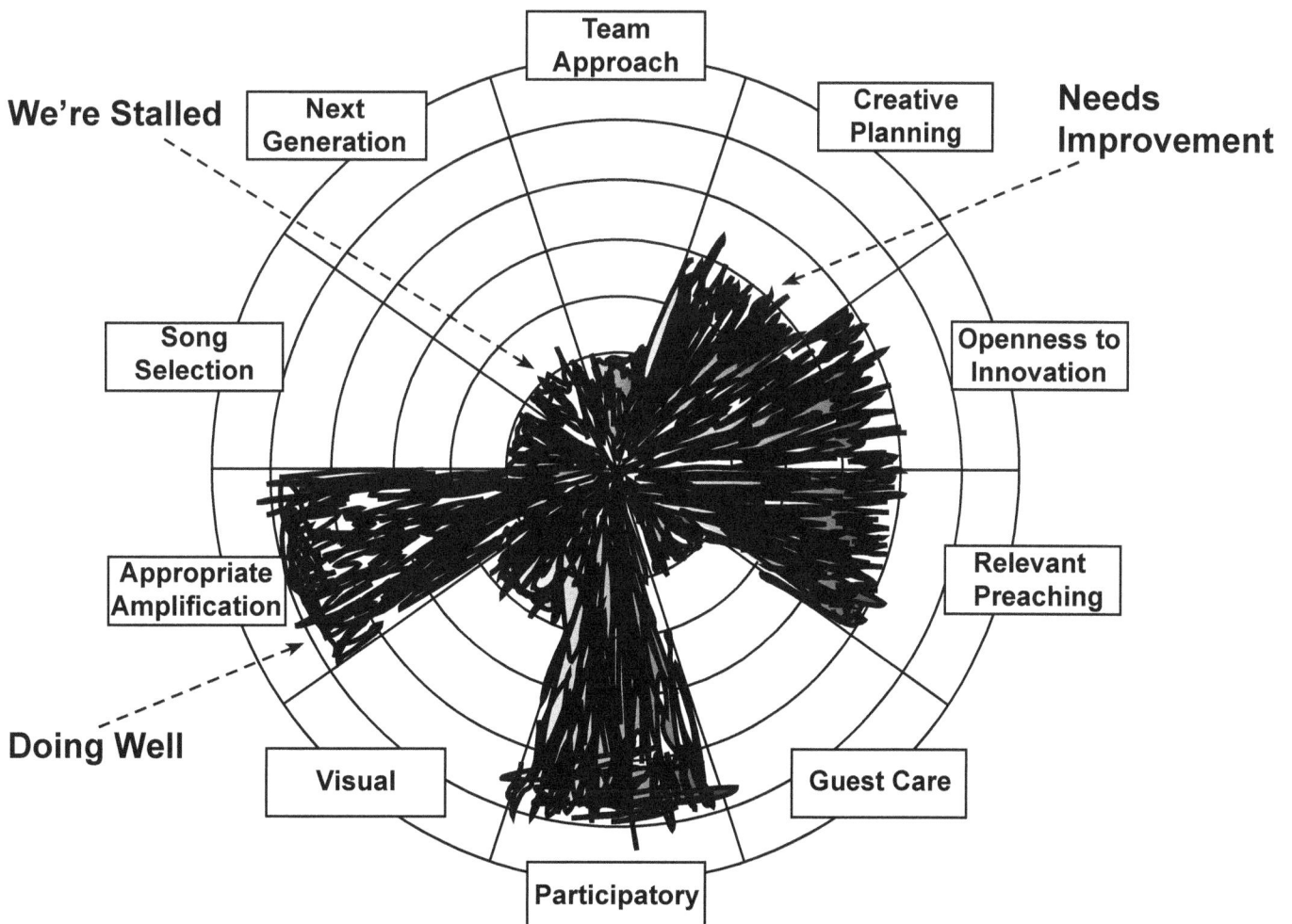

My Assessment of our Worship Services

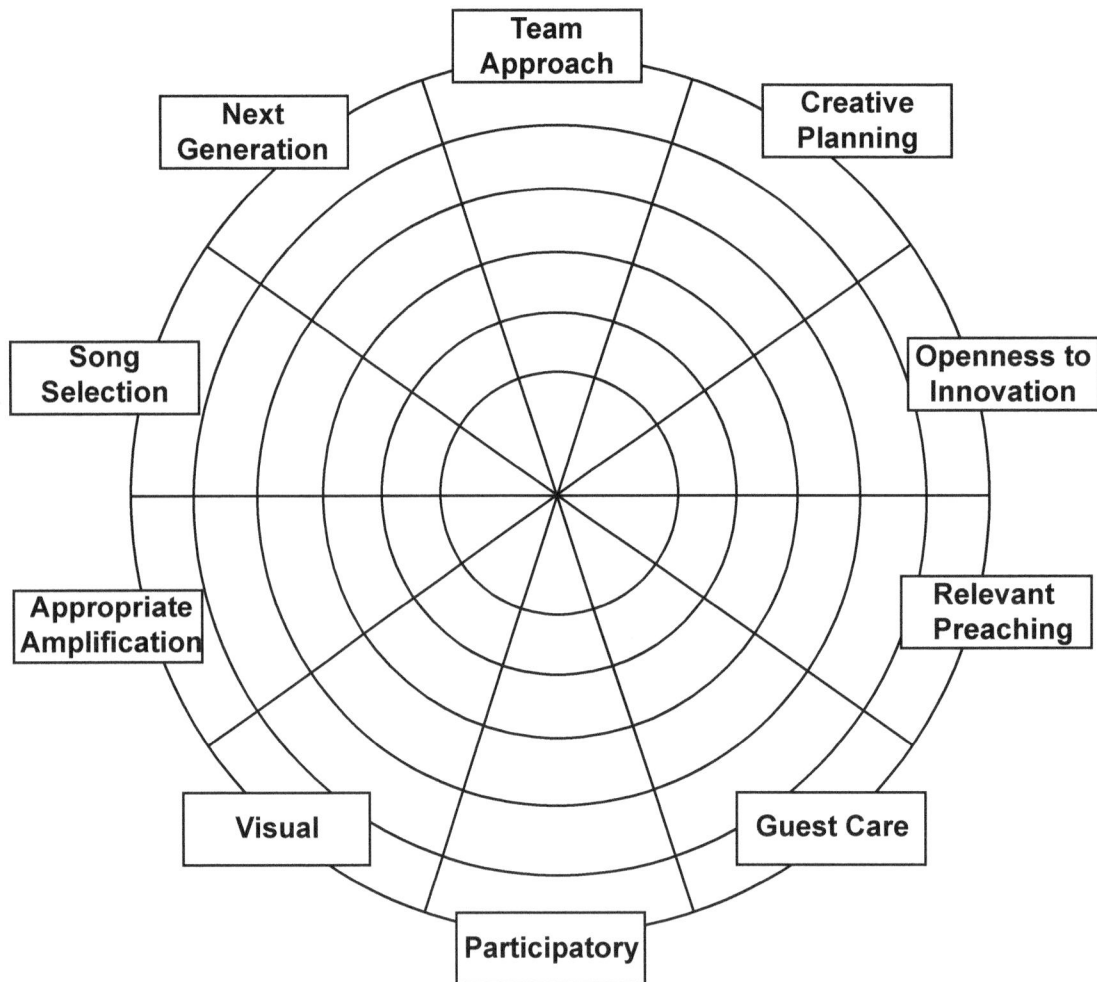

Assessment Reflection Questions

1	How can we use our strengths to address some of our lowest scores?	
2	Which key, if practiced consistently, would enable us to have more inspiring worship?	
3	What issue(s) need to be addressed first to enable us to have more inspiring worship services?	
4	What implications does this have for my use of time, our priorities, and future planning?	

Inspiring Worship Plan

Instructions: Use the worksheet below to list specific actions you intend to take related to this Skill Builder, the reflection questions and the self-assessment.

Specific Action Step	When will we take this action?
1	
2	
3	
4	
5	
6	
7	
8	

Sample Hinge Factor Report

In what follows, you will find an example of a report provided to churches that complete the TCN Church Assessment. The eight factors measured by this assessment correspond with the eight skills that are the focus of this *Skill Builders* workbook. When a church participates in this assessment, the report can greatly enhance the work and planning that results from this workbook.

Thank you for your participation in the Transforming Churches Network Hinge Factors Assessment. We appreciate the input from you and your congregation! This study is an effort to gain further insight into how TCN churches are doing with respect to best practices that impact our communities for Christ. We know that it is God's work alone that brings men and women to faith; however, we are His messengers and have a role to play in sharing the facts of His love and grace.

Your congregational members recently filled out the Hinge Factors questionnaire in which they rated your church and the pastor on a number of dimensions. These perceptions indicate how the laymen are experiencing the church, and often perception is reality. The graph below is a compilation of your scores and allows you to compare your scores to other churches who are engaged in the Transforming Churches Network initiative.

Overall Church Performance

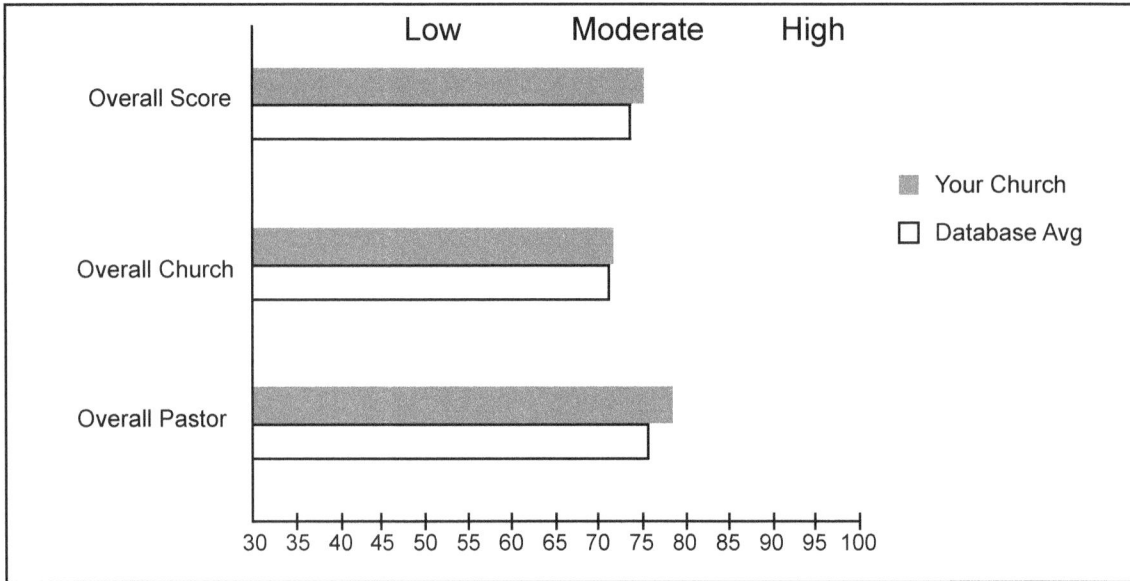

Reading the report: The rest of the report will give you a detailed description of the various dimensions of the questionnaire as well as specific help for interpreting your scores. For relative comparison purposes, also provided is the database average across all churches that have been measured to date. Bear in mind that your scores are compared across the total of all participants.

Pastor Factors: Your highest score on the Pastor Factors is Personal Leadership and your lowest score is Empowerment of Leaders.

Church Factors: Your highest score of the Church Factors is Inspiring Worship and your lowest score is Community Outreach.

Pastor Factors

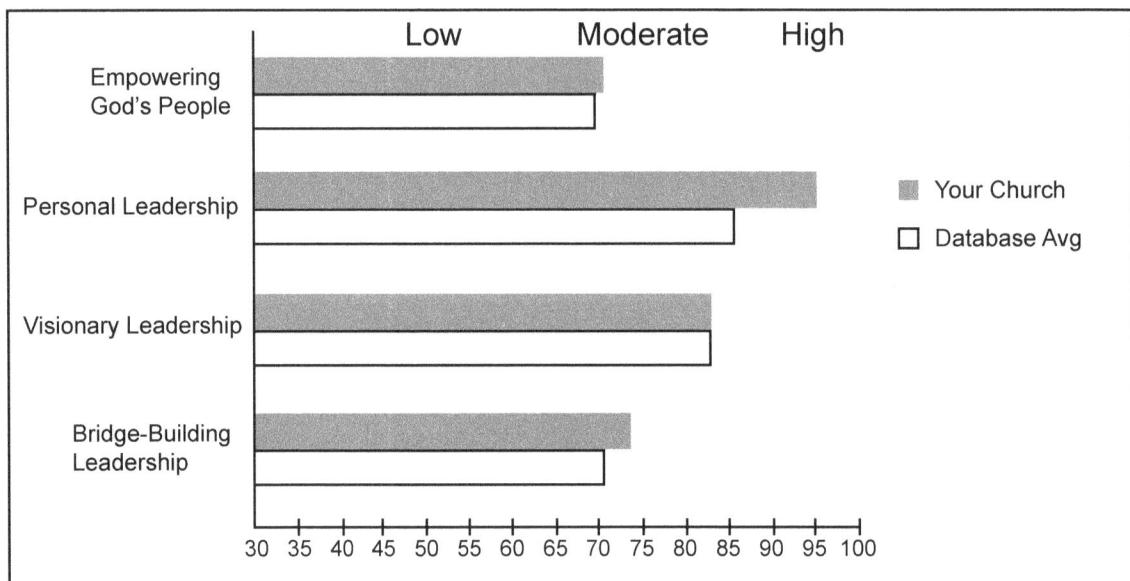

Pastor's Factor Chart

Our Score	What Our Score Possibly Indicates	Possible Next Steps
Empowering God's People *Moderate (69)*	*Metaphor: (Teacher)* Lay leaders are sharing the ministry load. There is an increasing need for the pastor to teach people about ministry leading.	1. Increase the amount of time each week devoted to coaching. 2. Launch a leadership training or development initiative.
Personal Leadership *High (93)*	*Metaphor: (8-Cylinder Engine)* The pastor models consistent personal balance. He has high levels of energy and is proactive in meeting the demands of ministry.	1. Increase the amount of time devoted to reflection and forward planning. 2. Engage a ministry coach 3. Find new ways to engage the community.
Visionary Leadership *Moderate (80)*	*Metaphor: (Bi-Focals)* Pastor is beginning to balance the internal care with the needs in the community.	1. Develop a ministry plan that has a few critical initiatives or projects for outreach. 2. Develop a strategy for helping long time members find ways to care for each other, releasing you to become mission oriented with your time.
Bridge-Building Leadership *Moderate (72)*	*Metaphor: (Feet are moving)* The pastor's feet are moving toward greater involvement in the community. He is connected to one or more needs in the community and is building greater rapport with those who need Christ.	1. Dedicate time blocks each week for your community involvement. 2. Increase your personal commitment to praying by name for those who need Christ.

Church Factors

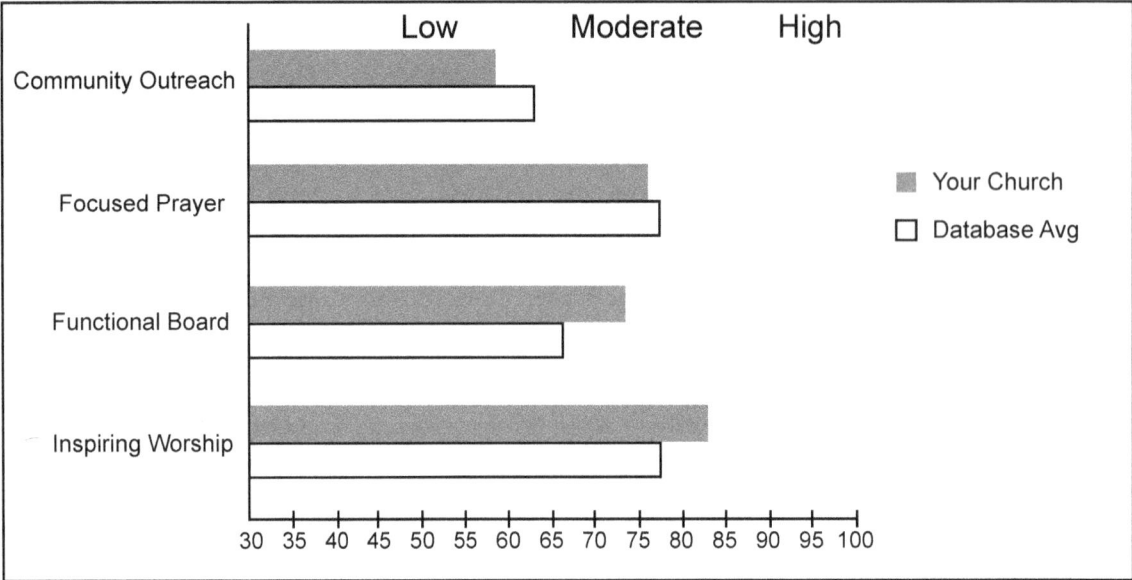

Low　　　　Moderate　　　High

- Community Outreach
- Focused Prayer
- Functional Board
- Inspiring Worship

■ Your Church
☐ Database Avg

30 35 40 45 50 55 60 65 70 75 80 85 90 95 100

Church Ministry Outcomes

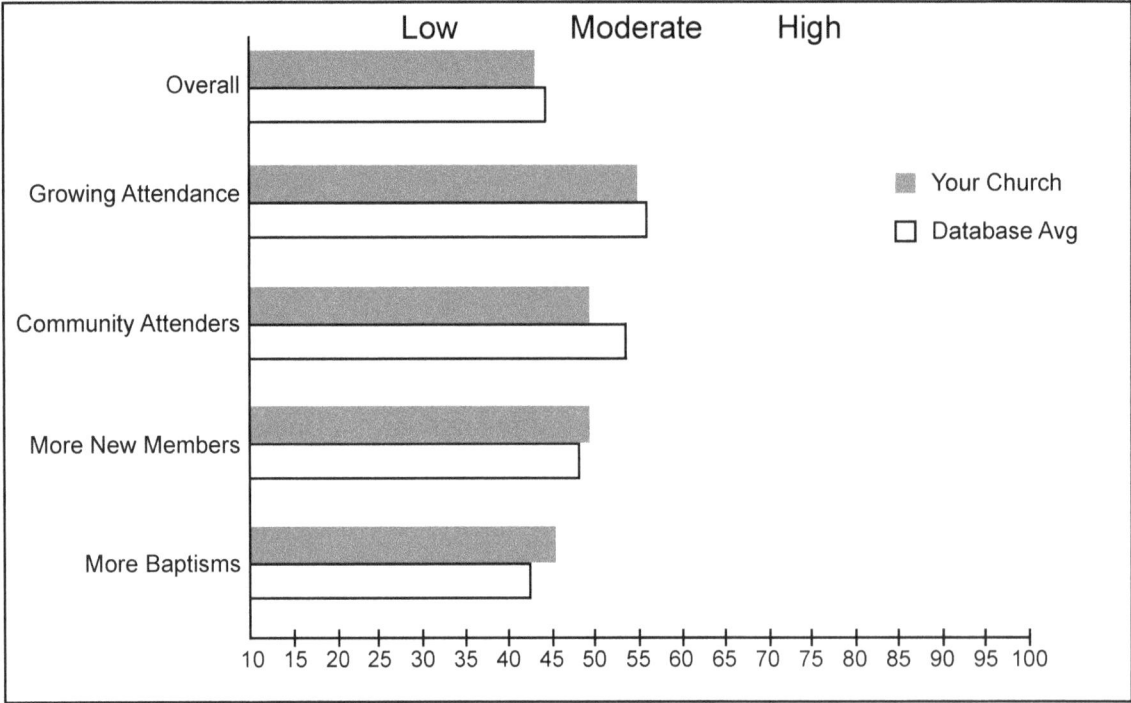

Low　　　　Moderate　　　High

- Overall
- Growing Attendance
- Community Attenders
- More New Members
- More Baptisms

■ Your Church
☐ Database Avg

10 15 20 25 30 35 40 45 50 55 60 65 70 75 80 85 90 95 100

Church Factor Chart

Our Score	What Our Score Possibly Indicates	Possible Next Steps
Community Outreach *Low (58)*	*Metaphor: (Family)* The needs of the church family are what are most important. One or more initiatives are needed to begin mobilizing outreach into the community.	1. Enlist the help of your coach in developing 6 Net Fishing Events for the year. 2. Capitalize on Christmas and Easter to mobilize the church body to invite friends to church.
Focused Prayer *Moderate (76)*	*Metaphor: (Jack Hammer)* People in the congregation are growing in their conviction and practice of prayer. Prayer in small group gatherings takes on increasing importance.	1. Preach a sermon series on the importance of personal and corporate prayer. 2. Mobilize a Prayer Team 3. Organize prayer around each time of worship. 4. Focus prayer on those who need to know Christ.
Functional Board *Moderate (71)*	*Metaphor: (Laying tracks)* The board begins to make a shift from putting out fires to finding ways to help the structure support a vision for the future. Church leaders are beginning to work together toward a common goal. Outreach is clearly on the agenda.	1. If you have boards, work on bringing those boards together on one vision, which the Pastor establishes. 2. Ensure that outreach goals are predominate in each board or staff position's agenda. 3. Begin to evaluate effectiveness by measuring outcomes instead of just activities.
Inspiring Worship *Moderate (82)*	*Metaphor: (Log fire)* The atmosphere, music, preaching, and relational interactions have some measure of warmth and attraction.	1. Form a Worship team with the express purpose of making the Worship service more culturally friendly to the community. 2. Ask unchurched people in the community to visit and give you feedback on their worship experience.

Foundation of the Report

Pastor Metrics Terms

The Pastor Factor section is based on how the church members scored the pastor, relative to the following Four Dimensions:

Empowering God's People: The pastor is developing leaders through coaching, mentoring, and training.

Personal Leadership: The pastor demonstrates a commitment to his own physical, mental, spiritual, and relational needs.

Visionary Leadership: The pastor creates a healthy sense of urgency about our ministry priorities and direction as a congregation.

Bridge-Building Leadership: The pastor dedicates some of his time towards connecting the church to the community.

Church Metrics Terms

The Church Factor section is based on how the church members scored your church, relative to the following Four Dimensions:

Community Outreach: A strategy for reaching the community is in place that results in increase in worship attendance.

Focused Prayer: An emphasis on prayer that incorporates intercession for those who need to know Christ.

Functional Board: A board that governs through Guiding principles and regular reviews of progress.

Inspiring Worship: A Worship Service where the preaching, music, and atmosphere attract more people from the community.

This study was based on over 1500 respondents across 44 churches. The factors reported in this study have been statistically assessed and higher scores on them link to an increase in baptisms and worship attendance. Understanding the interplay between the factors is important, as a high score on one or two factors does not necessarily indicate a growing church. As in any dynamic, living organism, the context in which the church exists, as well as other factors not measured by this study may have a significant impact on the growth of the church.

Please use the results of this project as an indicator of some of your strengths and areas of concern. We would encourage the pastor to work with his coach in finding creative ways to strengthen the areas of concern and also continue to grow in areas of strength. Prayer is consistently a way to strengthen what the Lord is doing in our churches and is critical as we reach out to those who do not know Christ.

One of the key ways that TCN seeks to strengthen the pastor and congregation in reaching their communities with the love of Christ is through the support provided by the coach. Pastor, coach and congregation can reflect on the findings of this survey and find focus and direction for the moving the congregation from in inward focused church to one that is focused on those who need to know Christ.

The missional opportunities in your community are abundant, whether a geographical community, a community of social networks, or both. "I tell you, open your eyes and look at the fields! They are ripe for harvest." John 4:35 (NIV) We understand that it is a process to learn how to find that ripe harvest, communicate vision, empower the church to reach out, and develop a church that is faithful to pray, reach, serve and share the message of Christ's love. Our goal is to help you and your congregation to succeed in that process.

www.ingramcontent.com/pod-product-compliance
Lightning Source LLC
Chambersburg PA
CBHW062051090426

42740CB00016B/3097